CU00485368

Stoke Field

'*I am afeard there are few die well that die in a battle; for how can they charitably dispose of any thing when blood is their argument.*'
William Shakespeare, *Henry V*, Act 4, Sc. 1

Stoke Field

The Last Battle of the Wars of the Roses

David Baldwin

Pen & Sword
MILITARY

First published in Great Britain in 2006 by
Pen & Sword Military
an imprint of
Pen & Sword Books Ltd
47 Church Street
Barnsley
South Yorkshire
S70 2AS

Copyright © text David Baldwin 2006.

Unless otherwise stated, all photographs in the plate section are © Geoffrey
Wheeler. All text figures are © Geoffrey Wheeler.

ISBN 1–84415–166–2

The right of David Baldwin to be identified as Author
of this Work has been asserted by him in accordance
with the Copyright, Designs and Patents Act 1988.

A CIP catalogue record for this book is
available from the British Library

All rights reserved. No part of this book may be reproduced or transmitted in
any form or by any means, electronic or mechanical including photocopying,
recording or by any information storage and retrieval system, without
permission from the Publisher in writing.

Typeset in 11/13 Ehrhardt by Concept, Huddersfield, West Yorkshire
Printed and bound in England by CPI UK

Pen & Sword Books Ltd incorporates the imprints of Pen & Sword Aviation,
Pen & Sword Maritime, Pen & Sword Military, Wharncliffe Local History,
Pen & Sword Select, Pen & Sword Military Classics and Leo Cooper.

For a complete list of Pen & Sword titles please contact
Pen & Sword Books Limited
47 Church Street, Barnsley, South Yorkshire, S70 2AS, England
E-mail: enquiries@pen-and-sword.co.uk
Website: www.pen-and-sword.co.uk

Contents

List of Illustrations

List of Maps

List of Plates

(between pages 78–9)

Modern memorial stone, St Oswald's church, south wall of tower

St Oswald's church, East Stoke

Willow Rundle, the 'well' of Stoke battlefield

Fiskerton, viewed from the Stoke bank of the River Trent

Human remains found south of the village in 1982 (Nottinghamshire County Council Historic Environment Record), and engraving of spur found on the battlefield *c.* 1825

Minster Lovel Hall and (insets) Lovel fording the Trent and the skeleton in the vault (artist's impressions)

York, Lancaster & Tudor

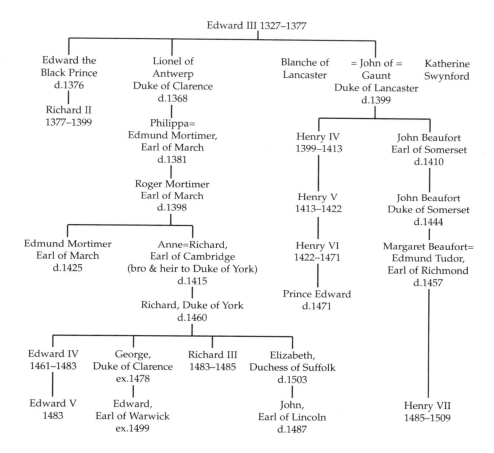

Edward III 1327–1377

Edward the Black Prince d.1376
  Richard II 1377–1399

Lionel of Antwerp Duke of Clarence d.1368
  Philippa= Edmund Mortimer, Earl of March d.1381
  Roger Mortimer Earl of March d.1398

Blanche of Lancaster   = John of = Katherine Swynford
Gaunt Duke of Lancaster d.1399

Henry IV 1399–1413
  Henry V 1413–1422
  Henry VI 1422–1471
  Prince Edward d.1471

John Beaufort Earl of Somerset d.1410
  John Beaufort Duke of Somerset d.1444
  Margaret Beaufort= Edmund Tudor, Earl of Richmond d.1457

Edmund Mortimer Earl of March d.1425

Anne=Richard, Earl of Cambridge (bro & heir to Duke of York) d.1415
  Richard, Duke of York d.1460

Edward IV 1461–1483
  Edward V 1483

George, Duke of Clarence ex.1478
  Edward, Earl of Warwick ex.1499

Richard III 1483–1485

Elizabeth, Duchess of Suffolk d.1503
  John, Earl of Lincoln d.1487

Henry VII 1485–1509

Introduction

The battle of Stoke, the last – and perhaps least known – conflict of the Wars of the Roses, is undoubtedly one of history's might-have-beens. The engagement, fought on Saturday 16 June 1487 between the forces of King Henry VII and a rebel army commanded by John de la Pole, Earl of Lincoln, Richard III's nephew, lasted for longer, and claimed many more victims, than the more famous battle of Bosworth two years earlier, but did not result in the death of a king or a change of dynasty. It has therefore been largely disregarded, although the situation in 1487 mirrored the unlikely circumstances in which Henry had destroyed Richard and the former might now have fallen victim to his own strategy. For the second time in under two years a rebel army, stiffened with a substantial number of foreign mercenaries, confronted a recently crowned king in the very heart of his kingdom, and the crisis of loyalty which paralysed the royal army at Bosworth was matched by an equally dangerous crisis of confidence among the Tudor forces before Stoke. There was one crucial difference: King Henry, rightly, gave priority to his own safety, while his rivals, more impetuous, lost both their lives and their cause. But it is likely that, had Lincoln won, Bosworth and the Tudor dynasty would have been relegated to a footnote of history, and the House of York would have governed for many more years.

Stoke Field has been considered by a number of battlefield historians, Richard Brooke and Colonel Alfred Burne[1] among them, but it was not until the quincentenary of the engagement in 1987 that its wider ramifications were studied in detail. A full length account of the Simnel rebellion by Dr Michael Bennett of the University of Tasmania was complemented by several booklets written by local historians,[2] and some readers may wonder why a new assessment is needed less than twenty years later. One reason is that a number of important books and articles dealing with the background to the uprising, and particularly its more regional aspects, have been published since 1987,[3] and another is that the work of Peter Newman and others has created a new discipline for the investigation and reconstruction of ancient battles which has not previously been applied to Stoke. I also wanted to go beyond the previous studies and discover why men were prepared to risk everything to help an obvious impostor rather than accommodate themselves to the new government. The old arguments that they fought because they were partisans of York or

Lancaster, or because of their traditional allegiance to the Neville family, seemed less than satisfactory; and it was evident that some who joined the rebels had local differences with Tudor supporters and they with them. Those who had finished on the losing side at Bosworth now faced a bleak future, and it seemed that only Henry's overthrow could produce a national government more to their liking and, more importantly, remove personal enemies who enjoyed his favour. Defeat meant disaster, but victory would restore them to positions of authority within their regions as the loyal and valued servants of a new Yorkist king.

This, then, will be a story of people as well as an account of a military conflict, and I looked for an individual whose life would act as a focus for the whole narrative. Like Barbara Tuchman, I wanted 'a male member of the second estate', i.e. a nobleman,[4] and have chosen Francis, Baron, later Viscount, Lovel, who was probably Richard III's closest friend and whose recorded career (1456–1487) spanned nearly the entire Wars of the Roses. No Lovel family archive has survived and a conventional biography is impossible. But there are documents which cast light on him in other collections, and many of these relate – or can be related – to the events of 1486–7. His devotion to the Yorkist kings – and consistent opposition to Henry VII – make him a better vehicle for our purposes than others who were prepared to temporise or whose support for the Simnel rebellion is at best conjectural, and it is likely that he was in no small measure responsible for what, for Henry, was an uncomfortably close call.

No account of a medieval battle can claim to be definitive or the last word on the subject, but I have tried to provide a better understanding of the events leading to the conflict (correcting some mistakes and misapprehensions in the process),[5] and to offer what I hope will prove to be a more accurate assessment of what happened on Stoke Field. The gaps in our knowledge have often been filled by speculation leading to differing interpretations, and there are still occasions when a choice has to be made between alternatives for which we possess little or no firm evidence. There are several conflicting versions of the route to Stoke taken by the rebels and the positions which the rival armies subsequently adopted on the battlefield (to mention just two examples), and I judged that there was no merit in simply repeating them. What I have tried to do is to distil what, on the balance of probability, seems to me to be the most likely scenario, and to give my reasons for preferring it. Alternative versions are noticed principally in the Notes and References section, and readers can study these and compare them if they wish.

Acknowledgements

I would like to thank Rupert Harding for inviting me to undertake the book and for his continuing interest in it, Virginia Baddeley (Sites & Monuments Record Officer, Nottinghamshire County Council) and Mark Dorrington (Principal Archivist, Nottinghamshire Archives) for providing information and answering queries. I am particularly grateful to Glenn Foard (Project Officer of the Battlefields Trust) for allowing me to read and use the unpublished report of his preliminary survey of the battlefield of Bosworth, and to Geoffrey Wheeler for reading my manuscript, providing the maps and some of the illustrations and (with C.E.J. Smith) seeking out many obscure details. And lastly (as always) I would like to thank my wife, Joyce, for sharing her thoughts during several visits to the battlefield and for helping in many other ways.

David Baldwin
July 2005

Chapter 1

Prelude to Conflict:
The Wars of the Roses

The battle of Stoke was the culmination of a series of conflicts which convulsed England in the latter half of the fifteenth century and which Sir Walter Scott called the 'Wars of the Roses'.[1] There were three distinct phases: from 1452 to 1464, from 1469 to 1471, and from 1483 to 1487, all related and interconnected, but also separate in that particular factors were responsible for each new outbreak. They differed from modern wars inasmuch as they were seldom continuous, and their effects varied considerably. It has been estimated that there were only some sixty-one weeks of domestic campaigning (in total) between 1455 and 1485,[2] and that most ordinary people were unaffected unless they happened to live near to a route taken by one of the armies. But four kings, Henry VI, Edward IV, Edward V and Richard III, were deposed (at least one, and possibly three, of them also died violently), and the leading noble families were decimated through two, or as many as three, generations. Overall, they claimed the lives of a larger proportion of the population of England than any conflict before the First World War.

The origins of the Wars of the Roses lay in the Hundred Years' War fought between England and France in the fourteenth and early fifteenth centuries. Henry V won glory at Agincourt and, ultimately, an empire which included large areas of France north of the River Loire: but he bequeathed an impossible legacy to his infant son and successor when he died prematurely in 1422. Henry VI was neither a warrior nor a statesman; and although the late King's brother, John, Duke of Bedford, secured and even extended the English position in the short term, he could do nothing to prevent the tide turning after Joan of Arc rallied the demoralised Dauphin and his armies in 1429. By the 1440s there was already conflict between a section of the English nobility who had profited from the war and who wanted to defend all the hero-king's conquests, and others who favoured rapprochement and the ceding of territory in return for a truce, or treaty, which would leave England with at least some possessions on the French side of the Channel. Both were unrealistic. The 'war' party failed to appreciate that the French, with their vastly greater resources, were bound to drive the English out eventually; and the 'doves' were mistaken if they thought that the French would rest until they had regained all the lands lost earlier in the century. It was the latter group which dominated the Council, however, and in 1445 they arranged for Henry VI to marry the French princess Margaret of Anjou in return for a truce of two years duration and the dim prospect of a permanent peace. The accord was extended when Henry and his ministers agreed to surrender Maine three years later; but a rash attack on the city of Fougères in March 1449 gave the French an excuse to break the agreement and the English armies were driven from Normandy within the year.

The ending of the war and the preservation of at least some of Henry V's conquests into the 1450s would have been regarded as a triumph of diplomacy for the court party, but the policy of détente had proved a failure and those who had pursued it were held to blame. William de la Pole, Duke of Suffolk, who had negotiated the King's marriage, and Edmund Beaufort, Duke of Somerset, who had commanded in northern France, were the inevitable scapegoats, and although Henry banished Suffolk to prevent his conviction, he was seized and murdered as he left the country. Jack Cade's rebellion, which broke out in May 1450, again emphasised the financial and military mismanagement of the King's favourites, and focused attention on the effective leader of the 'war' party, Richard, Duke of York. York, who was the childless King's heir-presumptive, had been consigned to the political wilderness in Ireland in 1449, and now benefited from the belief that the disaster in France would have been averted if he had been allowed his rightful place in the royal counsels. He returned to England in September 1450 and his demands for change led to Somerset being sent to the Tower; but Henry thought it unjust that his ministers should be prosecuted for pursuing policies which enjoyed his approval and the charges foundered. There was no concept of loyal opposition in the fifteenth century, and York could not challenge the court circle without appearing to threaten the king they served.

Somerset's release symbolised York's failure, but the loss of much of English Gascony in 1451 allowed him to renew his demands for change. He declared his loyalty to Henry while simultaneously raising an army which would compel the King to accept his arguments, and confronted the royal forces at Dartford, in Kent, in February 1452. There was no battle, however. York may have had the larger army, but was obliged to recognise that Henry still commanded the allegiance of most of the nobility, who made no distinction between a 'loyal' rebellion and treason. The King generously agreed to overlook the uprising in return for assurances of future fidelity, and York was allowed to retire to his estates.

The Duke had been fortunate to escape so lightly from Dartford, but may not have appreciated the King's leniency. He probably felt rejected and humiliated, and drew comfort from a violent feud which developed between his brother-in-law, Richard Neville, Earl of Salisbury and Warden of the West March towards Scotland, and the family of Salisbury's northern rival, Henry Percy, Earl of Northumberland. Salisbury and his son Richard Neville, Earl of Warwick (the future 'Kingmaker') had supported the King at Dartford, and doubtless believed they deserved royal favour. But the Percys were as close, perhaps even closer, to Henry, and the Nevilles increasingly identified themselves with York. An able king would have taken steps to prevent the emergence of distinctive pro- and anti-court factions; but crucially, Henry VI now lost his reason and firm government became impossible. The lords of the Council found themselves in the invidious position of having to continue the Crown's business without the right to take executive decisions or make policy. They could – and would – do those things which they were sure would meet with the King's approval when he recovered, but were inhibited by the fear that they would be accused of usurping his authority if he subsequently disagreed. Somerset and his friends tried to conceal Henry's illness, hoping, no doubt, that he would come to his senses; but his continuing incapacity precipitated a power-struggle which culminated in York's appointment as Protector in March 1454. Salisbury became chancellor, Somerset was again sent to the Tower, and an uprising by the Percys acting in concert with the Duke of Exeter (a son of Henry IV's sister, Elizabeth) was firmly dealt with. But Henry regained his sanity the following January, and dismissed York and Salisbury and their supporters. He was probably surprised to find Somerset and Exeter, who were among his closest relatives and confidants, in custody, and rapidly restored them to favour and power.

York's protectorate had provided him with a legal and constitutional outlet for his ambitions, and his dismissal was a blow to both his pride and his pocket. He could not influence events, still less recover the large sums he had spent in France in the 1440s, unless he enjoyed regular access to Henry, and the birth of the Prince of Wales on 13 October 1453 had seriously damaged his longer-term prospects. The Nevilles, too, stood to lose the advantages they had gained under the protectorate, and the three lords began to raise forces designed to force Somerset and the other courtiers who opposed them from office. The King summoned them to a meeting of the Great Council to be held at Leicester on 21 May 1455, and they encouraged him to think they would attend and wait upon him. But when Henry marched out of London en route for Leicester he found them drawn up in force at St Albans. Negotiations were conducted through heralds, York acting for the rebels and Humphrey Stafford, Duke of

Buckingham, for the court party. York demanded rapid (and favourable) answers to his petitions, and when Henry and his ministers failed to respond either rapidly or favourably, the Yorkists attacked. The outcome was never in doubt. Henry had about 2,000 people with him, but they included clerks, servants and others unprepared for battle. The rebel force was larger, well equipped, and more professional, and in a short, sharp fight in the streets of St Albans slew Somerset, Northumberland, his associate Lord Clifford, and about fifty others. Henry, slightly wounded by an arrow, sought refuge either in the abbey or a local tanner's cottage; and it was in one of these that the Yorkist lords found him and assured him of their loyalty! They had triumphed for the moment, but at what cost to noble unity and to the sanctity of this – or another – king?

The difference between 1455 and 1452 or even 1450 was that the Yorkists had used violence rather than merely threatened it, and had not only attacked the King but had risked killing him by firing arrows. It was perhaps the Nevilles, and Warwick in particular, who contributed the element of ruthlessness which had been missing from York's earlier confrontations with authority, and the belief of some royalists that the rebels would not commit treason by attacking them was a serious error. King Henry now had little alternative but to accept the Yorkist lords as his principal ministers, and when his illness recurred in October it was York who again became protector. The Duke tried to improve the royal finances by proposing the resumption (i.e. the cancellation and recovery) of many fees and annuities previously granted to individuals, and by restricting the income of the Queen, Prince and other members of the royal family. But there was widespread opposition (many of the annuitants were men of substance), and York found that it was by no means easy to pursue the 'right' policies while retaining the approval of the great and the good!

King Henry had recovered sufficiently to reclaim his authority by February 1456, and seems to have genuinely forgiven the Yorkist lords for their behaviour at St Albans. There were no abrupt dismissals (York ceased to be protector but remained chief councillor), and his friends kept the positions they had occupied since the previous summer. They may have convinced themselves that they were the King's true liegemen, but their opinion was not shared by everyone. Exeter remained a potentially dangerous opponent, Queen Margaret was concerned for Prince Edward, and the sons of Somerset, Northumberland and Clifford wanted revenge for their fathers' murders. An attempt to seize the Earl of Warwick in November was followed by an attack on York at Coventry, and Henry responded by summoning the parties to meet him at Westminster in January 1458. He brokered an agreement which required York to compensate Somerset's widow and son Henry (who had succeeded his father as duke), while Warwick made similar reparations to the new Lord Clifford; and they sealed the accord by processing to St Paul's Cathedral on the feast of the Annunciation of the Blessed Virgin (25 March), Salisbury walking with Somerset, Warwick with Exeter, and York with the Queen.

The 'Loveday' (as it is known), should have marked the beginning of a new chapter in relations between the former adversaries, partly because concord was clearly to everyone's advantage and because the award imposed large, potentially ruinous, penalties on any who flouted it. The Yorkists founded a chantry for the slain in St Albans Abbey (honouring another of the undertakings they had given), and appeared genuinely committed to the process of reconciliation; but they had become accustomed to dominating the government during the King's illness and found it difficult to accept a lesser role. They continued to dabble in foreign policy, and it was perhaps for this, or perhaps for other, now unknown, offences, that they were again indicted in the Parliament which met at Coventry in July 1459. Buckingham and other lords begged the King not to pardon them, but they were allowed to swear allegiance and provide sureties for their future conduct. They were permitted to retain their appointments and retired to their strongholds, York to Ludlow, Salisbury to Middleham and Warwick to Calais, to consider their response to their unjust treatment (as they perceived it) and the promises extracted from them under duress.

The armed challenge which the Yorkist lords mounted in September followed a familiar pattern and reiterated many of the arguments they had used in past uprisings. They were, they maintained, loyal subjects, the King's 'loveres', who, quite reasonably, sought to clear their names and reform the government and royal finances. They wanted to explain themselves to him, and only came in force because (they said), they could not trust the malicious courtiers who hated them and hoped to profit from their downfall. Much of this is disingenuous. The King's finances had already been reformed by the partial resumption (nothing could disguise the fact that his resources could not, and did not, meet his commitments), and it was little short of remarkable that he had again managed to surround himself with a group of councillors who were as 'evil' as those slain at St Albans. The Yorkists never recognised that they were subjects engaged in an armed, treasonable rebellion against their sovereign – or that their 'solution', that they should replace the existing government, was unacceptable to the wider political community. They passed almost imperceptibly from *coups d'état* to civil war.

The rebels' plan was to raise reliable forces in their respective heartlands and then unite to regain the dominance they had achieved at St Albans. They did not want to fight the King, still less depose him, but were determined to compel him to accept their particular view of the situation. Salisbury moved through Cheshire, intending to link up with York at Ludlow, but was intercepted by a contingent of the royal army at Blore Heath, near Market Drayton, on 23 September. The victory fell to the Yorkists, and although Salisbury was able to continue his journey, he was proclaimed a traitor. This was critical. Well-wishers who had accepted the rebel lords' argument that they were loyal to the Crown and desired only the common good could not ignore a royal edict to the contrary; and although Warwick duly joined his father and uncle at Ludlow they found themselves hemmed in by royal forces and unable to recruit. It was unrealistic to hope that even committed supporters would abet treason, and although Henry again offered to pardon them they fled, York to Ireland, and Salisbury, Warwick and York's eldest son, Edward, Earl of March, to Calais. Their going was incongruous, but the manner of it proclaimed both their continuing opposition and their intention to return.

Salisbury, Warwick and March landed at Sandwich on 26 June 1460, gathered forces in Kent (the lords and gentry of the south-eastern shires proved unable or unwilling to resist them), and were admitted to London. Henry had been obliged to spread his forces thinly – his enemies could have attacked almost anywhere – and now summoned them to meet him at Northampton. Mobilisation was a ponderous and time-consuming process, however, and the royal army was still assembling when the Yorkists, led by March and Warwick, arrived at the town on 10 July. They hoped to present their petitions to Henry personally, but their request for an audience was rejected by Buckingham, who again acted as the King's spokesman. He probably thought that nothing short of capitulation would satisfy them, and feared that he would be among the royal councillors to be removed and punished if Henry received them back into favour. The Yorkists quickly overwhelmed the smaller royal army – Buckingham, the Earl of Shrewsbury, and Lord Egremont, a son of the Earl of Northumberland, perished – and the King again fell into their hands.

Northampton was virtually a re-run of what had occurred at St Albans, and again, the Yorkist lords treated Henry respectfully and assured him of their loyalty. They secured the reversal of the attainders passed against them after their flight from Ludlow, but still faced serious opposition from Somerset, Exeter, Northumberland, Clifford, the Earl of Pembroke (the King's half-brother), and not least Queen Margaret and Prince Edward. Historians have long argued over when, and to what extent, Margaret opposed York and his supporters. The traditional view is that she hated them for the deaths of her friends at St Albans and perhaps blamed York for Suffolk's murder in 1450;

but a recent study suggests that she continued to use her influence as queen to mediate and became their enemy only after the failure of the 'Loveday' of 1458.[3] Warwick and Salisbury anticipated that a third protectorate would be established when York returned from Ireland; but when the Duke finally reached London in October he astounded everyone by claiming that he, and not Henry, was the rightful king. He argued that his descent from Lionel of Antwerp, Duke of Clarence, an elder son of Edward III, gave him precedence over Henry whose ancestor was Lionel's younger brother John of Gaunt, Duke of Lancaster; but the succession could be determined by factors other than nearness of blood or primogeniture, and the nobility refused to depose an anointed sovereign who had reigned over them for thirty-eight years. There was a furious row between York and Warwick, who feared that their previous assurances that they only wanted to reform the King's government would be condemned as fraudulent, and it was Warwick who arranged a compromise whereby Henry would remain king while he lived. York would be appointed protector (Henry would no longer have the power to dismiss him), and York and his sons would succeed to the throne on Henry's death.

It may be worth pausing for a moment to ask just how valid York's claim to the kingdom really was. His case was that the childless Richard II's rightful heir was his (Richard's) nearest male relative, Edmund Mortimer, Lionel of Clarence's great-grandson, and that Mortimer had been unjustly deprived of the succession when Henry VI's grandfather, Henry Bolingbroke, usurped the throne in 1399. If Henry IV ought not to have reigned, Henry V and Henry VI had no right to the crown either, and it was York, Mortimer's heir, who ought to be king. It was not quite that simple, however. Anointing and sacring had conferred legitimacy on rulers since Old Testament times, and more recent precedent had established that a king's eldest son was entitled to succeed him. The three Henrys were lawful kings in the sense that they were all crowned and anointed, and Prince Edward was as entitled to succeed his father, Henry VI, as Henry VI and Henry V had succeeded theirs. Richard the Lionheart, the last English king to die childless, had been succeeded by his brother John rather than by his nearest male relative, his nephew Arthur; but York argued that his 'hereditary right' took precedence over all other considerations. Protests that he had borne the arms of York, his father's family, rather than those of his mother's Clarence ancestors, through whom he now claimed the Crown, were dismissed as abruptly as the objection that Parliament had settled the Crown on the House of Lancaster – the Duke wished to believe what he wished to believe.

The agreement between York and Warwick may have satisfied the peers based in London, but it was wholly unacceptable to Queen Margaret, who was determined to protect her son's inheritance. She gathered forces in northern England and was joined by West Countrymen led by the Dukes of Somerset and Exeter and by the Earl of Devon who had married her cousin Marie of Maine. The Yorkists decided, rather imprudently, to divide their forces: Warwick was to remain in London while March dealt with Pembroke and the Welsh Lancastrians, and York and Salisbury marched northwards to confront Margaret. The Yorkists could again claim that they were acting on the King's behalf and with his approval, and York and Salisbury may have supposed that this would inhibit their enemies when they confronted them with a smaller army at Wakefield on 30 December. They were sadly mistaken. York's head, sporting a paper crown, was displayed on Micklegate Bar in York city after the battle, and Salisbury was killed by the commons at Pontefract a few days afterwards. The north was now Lancastrian territory although York held a northern title and both he and Salisbury drew much of their support from their northern lands.

Queen Margaret capitalised on her victory by marching south and defeating Warwick's forces at the second battle of St Albans (17 February 1461). She regained possession of her hapless husband, and the Yorkist lords turned to York's son Edward, who had vanquished the Welsh Lancastrians at Mortimer's Cross on 3 February. It was agreed that Warwick would promote Edward's candidacy for the throne (notwithstanding that he had refused to support his father's claim only five weeks earlier), and the new King was acclaimed by his supporters on 3 March. Margaret, meanwhile, had been obliged to retreat northwards – she was reluctant to attack and alienate London and could not keep her troops in the field indefinitely – and the Yorkists lost no time in pursuing her. They successfully forded the River Aire at Ferrybridge on 28 March, and next day, Palm Sunday, defeated the Lancastrian army at Towton in what was destined to be the bloodiest battle of the entire conflict. The victory proved decisive. The royal family, which had awaited news of the outcome at York, was able to retire to Scotland, but their exile prevented them from raising another substantial army even though Somerset, Exeter and other survivors remained committed to them. They secured foreign backing by surrendering Berwick to the Scots and promising Calais to the French (as and when they recovered it), but were confined to holding the great Northumbrian castles against Edward's armies and to making incursions by sea. Their small forces were destroyed at Hedgeley Moor and Hexham in April and May 1464 (Somerset was killed in the latter action), and when Henry was captured shortly afterwards Margaret and her son sought safety in France.

This first phase of the Wars of the Roses witnessed the births of several of those destined to be among the leading protagonists at Stoke some thirty years later. Henry Tudor, the future King Henry VII, was born in January 1457; John de la Pole, the eldest son of Edward IV's sister Elizabeth and the new Duke of Suffolk, between 1462 and 1464 (he was created Earl of Lincoln in 1467); and Francis Lovel in November 1456.[4] The Lovels were descended from William, Earl of Yvery, in Normandy and were first summoned to Parliament as barons (of Titchmarsh, in Northamptonshire) in 1297. They acquired wealth through royal service and marriages with heiresses, and when John Lovel, Francis's father, died in 1465 he held no fewer than three baronies (Lovel, Holand and Burnell) and would have inherited two others (Deincourt and Grey of Rotherfield) had he outlived his mother. He was one of several lords who tried to secure London for King Henry before the battle of Northampton and subsequently fought for him at Towton; but he bowed to the inevitable and had begun to receive minor appointments from King Edward by 1464. The King became Francis's guardian at his father's death, and used the opportunity to further reward Warwick and his connection. He was married to Warwick's niece, Ann Fitzhugh, before 17 February 1466 (probably not long after his ninth birthday), and custody of his estates and person was formally granted to the Earl in November 1467.[5] He had perhaps already commenced his knightly training at Middleham Castle, and may have encountered King Edward's youngest brother, Richard, Duke of Gloucester, who was four years his senior and also a member of Warwick's household. Their friendship blossomed – whether then or later is uncertain – and Francis, the son and grandson of Lancastrians, became a staunch supporter of the House of York.

Lovel's wardship and marriage was only one of many favours which King Edward bestowed on Warwick and the Nevilles, but they became progressively disillusioned with his government. Edward's secret marriage to an English gentlewoman, Elizabeth Woodville, while Warwick was negotiating for the hand of a French princess made the proud Earl appear foolish; and he undoubtedly felt thwarted when several valuable heirs and heiresses were given to members of the new Queen's family. Anne, the Duke of Exeter's daughter, who was to have married George, his nephew, was betrothed instead to Thomas Grey, Elizabeth Woodville's elder son by her first marriage, and the young Duke of Buckingham (the slain Duke's grandson) who, he hoped, would become the husband of Isabel, his elder daughter, was married to Catherine, one of the Queen's sisters. He may also have resented the King's very public dismissal of his brother, George, Archbishop of York, from the chancellorship in 1467, and Edward's decision to marry his sister Margaret to Charles, Duke of Burgundy, the King of France's independent-minded vassal, a year later. The knowledgeable Croyland chronicler thought that the Burgundian marriage was 'the real cause of dissension between the king and the earl',[6] but Warwick would surely have expected Edward to pursue his own policies as he gained in experience, however much he owed to him. It was more probably the friendship which had developed between Edward and some of the male Woodvilles – men who had fought for the House of Lancaster while Warwick had been winning England for the Yorkists – which made him feel ill-used and neglected. What right had the King to make these low-born former enemies his favourites, and what right had they to diminish Warwick's influence with the king he had created? The Earl decided to teach his former protégé a lesson and restore himself to what he regarded as his rightful place.

The years 1469 to 1471 witnessed the renewal of the Roses conflict and several quite remarkable changes of fortune. Warwick began by stirring up what is known as 'Robin of Redesdale's' rebellion in northern England in June 1469, and used 'Robin' to defeat a royal army led by the Earls of Pembroke and Devon at Edgecote, near Banbury, on 26 July. He executed several of his Woodville rivals and took Edward into custody at Middleham; but he quickly discovered that he could not rule through the King (few would respond to orders which did not genuinely come from Edward), and was obliged to set him at liberty. Edward did not charge Warwick with disloyalty (as he might well have done) and was prepared to let bygones be bygones; but the Earl had failed to recover his former influence and his thoughts turned to replacing Edward with his brother, George, Duke of Clarence. Warwick had married his daughter Isabel to Clarence shortly before Edgecote in defiance of the King's wishes and doubtless thought him more malleable than Edward; but the 'Lincolnshire Rebellion', which they fomented in March 1470, failed to repeat 'Robin of Redesdale's' successes. King Edward moved swiftly – and this time personally – to defeat the insurgents at the battle of Empingham (or 'Losecote Field'), and summoned Warwick and Clarence to appear before him. They declined to come however (their likely humiliation was probably more than they could contemplate), and instead sought refuge in France.

Their arrival presented the French king, Louis XI, with a golden opportunity to cause trouble in England, and at Angers on 22 July 1470 he brought Warwick face to face with his old enemy Queen Margaret and persuaded them to be friends. They agreed that the Earl would invade England with the avowed aim of restoring King Henry, and that Margaret's son, Prince Edward, would marry Anne, Warwick's younger daughter; but there was no mention of what would happen to lands held by Yorkists (by committed supporters like Clarence and others they hoped to win over), which had belonged to dispossessed Lancastrians before 1461. A rising in Richmondshire led by Henry, Lord Fitzhugh (Warwick's brother-in-law and Lovel's father-in-law) may have begun prematurely in late July, but it still ensured that King Edward was in the north when his enemies landed in the West Country on 13 September. Edward's problem was that his government had failed to fulfil popular expectations (little had been done to redress the grievances of the 1450s), and the defection of Warwick's hitherto loyal brother John Neville, Marquis Montague, proved decisive. Henry VI recovered his throne after a near ten-year interval, and Edward with a few companions found refuge in Holland.

Warwick's bloodless triumph mirrored his dramatic success at the battle of Northampton, but it was inevitable that Edward would try to reverse the situation. Duke Charles of Burgundy provided him with money and shipping, and his little party landed at Ravenspur, on the River Humber, on 14 March 1471. His proclamation that he came only to recover his father's duchy may have dissuaded Warwick's northern commanders, Montague and the Earl of Northumberland, from attacking him; and he was able to advance into the Midlands recruiting forces as he went. The overwhelming strength of his enemies could – and should – have destroyed him: but Warwick was at Coventry (which he declined to leave to fight Edward single-handedly), the Earl of Oxford and the Duke of Exeter were to the east of his army, and the Duke of Somerset and the Earl of Devon were in the West Country awaiting Queen Margaret's return from France. He received a major boost when Clarence, moved, perhaps, by a combination of family pressure and self interest, rejoined him outside Coventry; and the brothers marched swiftly on London where Edward was able to rescue his Queen and new-born son from sanctuary and again capture Henry VI. Warwick gathered the various strands of his forces and followed him, but on 14 April was decisively defeated by Edward's smaller army at Barnet. The King had matured into a better general than his teacher, although mistrust between traditional Lancastrians and their new Neville allies was a crucial element in his success.

News of the deaths of Warwick and Montague would have reached Queen Margaret soon after she landed at Weymouth on the day Barnet was fought, but she quickly raised a new army. She hoped to cross the River Severn and link up with supporters in Wales and northern England, but Edward's men held the bridges and her forces were cornered, exhausted, at Tewkesbury on 3 May. The Yorkist army had also been subjected to forced marches, but next day Edward won another crushing victory. Margaret was captured, her son fell in the pursuit, the Duke of Somerset (the third such to die for the House of Lancaster) was executed after being forcibly removed from the sanctuary of Tewkesbury Abbey, and Henry VI died suddenly in the Tower the night his enemies returned to London. The wars had now claimed not only the 'King-maker' but also a king.

Francis Lovel had only recently entered his teens and can have played no part in Lord Fitzhugh's rising in 1470, but he was included (together with his wife and two sisters) in the pardon granted to the family on 10 September, three days before Warwick reached England. The Earl had presumably allowed his young charge to live with the other children in the Fitzhugh household at Ravensworth, in Yorkshire, but the situation changed dramatically after he was killed at Barnet. Lovel was too valuable an heir to be left in the custody of a minor baron of uncertain loyalties, and his wardship was granted to the King's sister Elizabeth and her husband the Duke of Suffolk. He was probably unhappy to leave the north and the camaraderie of the Neville affinity, but his entry into the Suffolks' establishment brought him into contact with their eldest son, John. Nothing is known of their relationship, but it would not be remarkable if the young Earl of Lincoln came to like, even admire, the older boy who was to be his companion in arms on Stoke Field.

King Edward reigned for another twelve years after his victory at Tewkesbury, before dying, aged only 40, in April 1483. Lovel was allowed to enter his inheritance in November 1477, and was thereafter much in demand on Crown business. Appointments to commissions of the peace, array and *oyer et terminer* were followed by a royal summons to parliament, and he gained his first experience of campaigning when he invaded Scotland with Richard of Gloucester in 1482. Duke Richard knighted him 'at Hoton (Hutton) Field beside Berwick'[7] on 22 August (an ominous date for those who believe in such portents); and when the army returned to England after its prestigious – but inevitably temporary – capture of Edinburgh he was created Viscount Lovel by King Edward. He seemed set to enjoy a long career as a dependable member of the middling nobility, but Edward's death had far reaching consequences. Within three months Gloucester had outmanoeuvred his opponents to become king as Richard III, and Lovel found himself a senior member of the new government. His appointment as chamberlain meant that he had regular daily access to Richard as well as considerable influence over who did, or did not, see him; and there is no reason to doubt the substance of Colyngbourne's jibe that, together with Sir Richard Ratcliffe and William Catesby, he 'ruled all England under the Hog'.[8]

The Lovel family had resided principally at Minster Lovel in Oxfordshire since before the middle of the century, but Francis's responsibilities both in the north and as a courtier meant that he was seldom 'at home'. When the Duke of Buckingham, King Richard's erstwhile ally, rebelled against him in the late Autumn of 1483, Lovel wrote to Sir William Stonor, his principal agent in the county, instructing him to bring his company to Leicester where the royal army was mustering. He was painfully unaware that Stonor (together with

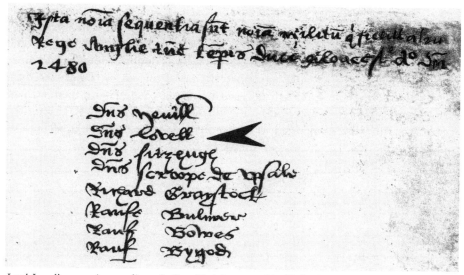

Lord Lovel's name (arrowed) on the list of knights created by Richard, Duke of Gloucester 'at Hoton Field beside Berwick' in 1480. (Redrawn from BL Harleian Roll E2)

numerous other southern gentlemen), had already joined the rebels; and although the uprising faltered it showed very clearly that both he and his royal master were regarded as 'alien' northerners rather than the leaders of a broadly representative government. They could do nothing to raise their popularity in the south in the short term (only time would have allowed them to overcome old prejudices and gain approval), nor could they prevent Henry Tudor, the last sprig of the House of Lancaster, from preparing to invade England from his base in France. In May 1485 Lovel was sent to Southampton to ready ships to resist Tudor if he should try to land in the vicinity; but he hurried back to join Richard at Bosworth when it became apparent that the enemy had decided to make his bid for the crown through Wales. King Richard ought not to have lost the battle of Bosworth – he was a more experienced general and had a much larger army – but the opposition was both desperate and determined and some of his supporters were apparently unwilling to fight for him. By the evening of 22 August his battered corpse was being carried to Leicester, Henry Tudor had become King Henry VII, and Lovel was a fugitive on England's roads.

King Richard's death was a bonus his enemies could not have expected (no English sovereign had been killed in battle since Hastings), and led to renewed hopes that the Wars were finally over. They had appeared to end at Towton in 1461 but had resumed eight years later; and although Barnet and Tewkesbury had all but destroyed the threat from both Warwick and the Lancastrians there had been more troubles when Edward IV died. Henry VII's marriage with King Edward's daughter Elizabeth was designed to heal the rift between the opposing factions, and the Croyland chronicler was doubtless expressing more than his own opinion when he described the new King as 'an angel sent from heaven through whom God had deigned to visit his people and to free them from the evils which had hitherto afflicted them beyond measure'.[9] Here, the writer thought, was a settlement which would endure because it was acceptable to nearly everyone.[10] But he was mistaken. Stoke Field lay ahead.

Chapter 2

The Lambert Simnel Conspiracy

Francis Lovel made his way to Colchester after the battle of Bosworth, where, with Sir Humphrey Stafford and his brother Thomas, he took sanctuary in the abbey of St John the Baptist. Their choice of refuge is puzzling – Colchester is nearly 200 miles from Leicester and the abbot, Walter Stansted, was not a noted Yorkist or Ricardian – and the only logical explanation is that they initially thought of crossing to Burgundy. The forty days during which sanctuary men were allowed to decide whether to surrender to justice or leave England came and went, however, and it became apparent that they were in no immediate danger. The new King may have lacked the physical resources to pursue and arrest them, and Lovel's extensive influence in both southern and northern England meant that he was the kind of man Henry would prefer to have working with him rather than against him. William Catesby, making his will three days after Bosworth, thought that Lovel would soon 'come to grace',[1] and Henry would not have appointed Richard, Lord Fitzhugh (the late Lord Henry's son and Francis's brother-in-law), to major offices in Richmond and Barnard Castle on 25 September if he thought the family beyond redemption. Many years later Sir Hugh Conway recounted how he had passed on reliable information that Lovel intended to leave Colchester and continue the struggle, but that the King had refused to believe it. Henry 'said that hyt could not be so, and resoned with me alwayes to the contrary of my said sayings.'[2] He was presumably both surprised and disappointed when it became apparent that Conway had spoken the truth.

King Henry left London with the approach of Easter 1486 intending to see, and be seen in, his newly conquered country. He passed Holy Week at Lincoln, where he was reliably informed that Lovel and the Stafford brothers had left sanctuary, although no one knew where they had gone. He continued his progress northwards via Nottingham, Doncaster and Pontefract, and it may have been at one of these places, or perhaps shortly after he reached York on about 20 April, that he heard that Lovel was raising forces in the vicinity of Middleham in north Yorkshire and that the Staffords were fomenting trouble in Worcestershire. Polydore Vergil, Henry's court historian, says that his master was 'struck by great fear'[3] because his men were not numerous and were ill-equipped to fight a battle. An attempt to capture the King in York was frustrated by the Earl of Northumberland,[4] and Henry seized the initiative by despatching the forces he had against the northern rebels with authority to offer pardon to all who would lay down their weapons. Lovel, apparently mistrusting the outcome, abandoned his followers to the royal mercy, and his failure precipitated the collapse of the plan to seize Worcester. Vergil calls Francis an 'irresolute fellow ... seized by groundless fear' who, because of 'feebleness of spirit'[5] had not dared risk combat; but a more likely explanation is that some of the support he had anticipated had not materialised, and it had become apparent that confrontation must be put off to another day.

Lovel must have hoped that many northerners who had served Richard III, both as king and as Duke of Gloucester, would rally to his standard, and it is worth asking why they apparently did not. The main reason was surely that Henry VII recognised that he could not rule the north without the help of many of those who had been on the losing side at Bosworth, and it was becoming apparent to them that they would be allowed to keep their positions in the localities. The Act of Attainder passed against the late King and his principal adherents in November 1485 punished the relatively small number of individuals named in it, but made it clear there would be no wider persecution.[6] Only eight knights were convicted: Sir Richard Ratcliffe of Derwentwater (Cumb.), Sir Richard Charlton of Edmonton (Middx), and Sir Robert Brackenbury of Denton (Durham), who had all been killed; Sir William Berkeley of Uley (Glos.), who was pardoned in June 1486;[7] and four northerners, who survived – Sir James Harrington of Brierley (Yorks.), his brother Sir Robert of Badsworth (Yorks.), Sir Thomas Pilkington of Pilkington (Lancs.), and Sir Robert Middleton of Dalton (Westmoreland). Even dedicated Ricardians like Sir Thomas Broughton of Broughton-in-Furness (Lancs.) and Sir John Huddleston of Millom (Cumb.) were not included, and they were far from being the exception. When Henry was progressing northwards in mid-April 1486 he was met south of Doncaster by the Earl of Northumberland and a large company of Yorkshire knights including four who had been retained by King Richard: Sir William Eure of Old Malton, Sir James Strangeways of West Harlsey, Sir Richard Conyers of South Cowton, and Sir Christopher Ward of Givendale, and five others who (in all probability) had joined him before Bosworth – Sir Thomas Mauleverer of Allerton Mauleverer, Sir Robert Plumpton of Plumpton, Sir William Gascoigne of Gawthorpe, Sir Robert Ughtred of Kexby and Sir Martin del See of Barmston.[8] Conyers and Ward were subsequently taken into custody and obliged to find sureties for their future behaviour (which implies that they were suspected of assisting Lovel or at least doing nothing to hinder him),[9] but the others remained loyal to the new government.[10] There is no evidence that the two Harringtons, Pilkington or Robert Middleton played any part in the uprising, and they were pardoned, together with Broughton, Huddleston, and several prominent Yorkshire esquires (including Geoffrey Frank of Escrick, John Ward of Ripon [Sir Christopher's brother], Thomas Otter of Middleham and Richard Middleton of Spofforth) in July and August.[11] Edward Frank of Knighton (Yorks.) seems to have been the only known dissident who was not forgiven and may well have joined Lovel; but many former Ricardians preferred to follow the example of Sir Ralph Bigod of Settrington (Yorks.), whose burgeoning career was interrupted by the battle of Bosworth but who found employment in the household of King Henry's mother, Lady Margaret Beaufort, before being appointed constable of Sheriff Hutton castle on 5 May 1486.[12] Self-aggrandisement was always a factor, and the more comfortable these men felt with Henry Tudor (and the greater their interest in his survival), the less likely they would be to rebel.

Polydore Vergil says that Lovel found refuge with Sir Thomas Broughton after the collapse of his uprising; but the Countess of Oxford had been 'credebly enfourmed' that he was in the Isle of Ely by 19 May. She instructed John Paston, recently appointed sheriff of Norfolk and Suffolk, to 'endevore that suche wetche (watch) or other meanes be used and hadde in the poorts and creks ... to the letting (hindering) of his seid purpose ... and to use all the waies ye can or maie by your wisdom, to the taking of the same Lorde Lovell'.[13] He remained at liberty for the rest of the year, however, and when Paston reported to the Earl of Oxford that he had slipped away with a number of followers at the beginning of January 1487, Oxford replied laconically that there was nothing new in his information and that he (Lovel) was only then departing 'with xiiii personys and no moe'.[14] His destination was Malines in the Burgundian Netherlands, the home of Duchess Margaret, Charles the Bold's widow and the Yorkist kings' sister. Margaret had lost valuable commercial privileges in England on Henry Tudor's accession, and naturally wished to recover them together with the unpaid balance of her dowry. She also shared the fears of her son-in-law, Archduke Maximilian, that the help Henry had received from France would lead to an Anglo–French attack on the Burgundian territories, and was ready to use her wealth and influence to promote the interests of her English family. It must have seemed that there was little prospect of toppling Henry in the near future, but Lovel encouraged her, in Vergil's words, 'to undertake more ambitious plans'.[15]

Precisely what these plans were will always be open to speculation, but there can be little doubt that Lovel had used the eight months which had elapsed between the failure of his uprising and his flight to the Netherlands well. It can hardly be coincidence that the two main centres of opposition to Henry in southern England – at Oxford and Abingdon – lay only sixteen or seventeen miles from his home at Minster Lovel, and there is every likelihood that he visited the area in the summer of 1486. He had helped to re-found the wealthy Fraternity of the Holy Cross at Abingdon two years earlier, and would have known the local abbot, John Sante. A prominent Yorkist, Sante had been on diplomatic missions for Edward IV, and had sheltered Humphrey Stafford in the abbey's sanctuary of Culham after the collapse of the rebellion in Worcester. He protested vigorously when Stafford was forcibly removed and subsequently executed, but his efforts only earned him a fine for assisting a traitor. He was probably angry and disillusioned when Lovel approached him, and although his role in the Simnel conspiracy is lost to history there is no reason to doubt that he was 'falsly and traiterously compassyng, conspiryng and ymaginyng the destruction of the King'[16] at the beginning of 1487.

Sante's assistance was financial rather than political however, and it was at nearby Oxford that the plot to challenge Henry was hatched. Polydore Vergil's version of the story is that a 'lowborn' scholar-priest, Richard Simons, had been entrusted with the upbringing of a personable youth named Lambert Simnel, and decided to teach him courtly manners so that he would be able to impersonate a Yorkist prince. His choice fell on Edward, Earl of Warwick, the Duke of Clarence's son, who was about the same age as Simnel and who had been imprisoned in the Tower since shortly after Bosworth. The pair went to Ireland where the House of York had been held in special affection since Duke Richard's lieutenancy in 1449–50, and there Simons 'secretly summoned a meeting of a considerable number of Irish nobles',[17] convinced them that his 'Earl of Warwick' was genuine, and raised the standard of revolt.

Vergil does not tell us exactly when these events happened; nor does he explain how a priest with (presumably) no knowledge of court life could teach a boy to behave like a prince or why the Irish nobles responded to his summons. Dr Bennett has pointed out that even his name is implausible – there are few Lamberts and fewer Simnels mentioned in medieval records, and the herald who accompanied the Tudor army to Stoke Field referred to him simply as 'John'. There may also have been two priests called Simons, Richard, who was captured with his protégé after the battle, and a William, perhaps his brother, who confessed before the Convocation of Canterbury in February 1487 that he had taken Simnel to Ireland but had then returned to England and had met Lovel in Lancashire, probably towards the end of 1486.[18] His purpose was evidently to report that the first stage of the plan had succeeded so that Lovel could cross to Burgundy to arrange matters there.

It is impossible to suggest why 'John' should have been called Lambert Simnel if his new identity was to be Edward, Earl of Warwick, but there is no reason to suppose that he was more than the son of a tradesman.[19] He must, however, have been trained and plausible when he was taken to Ireland, probably in the autumn of 1486, and was perhaps being coached before Lovel arrived in Oxford. It is likely that the Irish lords had entered into the conspiracy on the understanding that powerful figures in England would support them, and had agreed to take Simons and Simnel seriously before Simons issued his 'summons'. We do not know how this was accomplished, but it is possible that Lovel made contact with a number of prominent Yorkists in the course of his travels in the summer of 1486, and had won enough backing to convince the Irish peers by the early autumn. He cannot have pretended that Simnel was anything other than an impostor, but was able to persuade his allies that it would be easier to harness popular support for Warwick if he appeared to be with them in person. The substitute would, of course, be discarded when the real Earl was liberated and could take his place.

We know the names of most of the rebels because they subsequently joined the uprising and were slain or punished afterwards, but the identities of two of Lovel's contacts must be inferred from the action which Henry VII subsequently took against them. The first is Elizabeth Woodville, Edward IV's widow and the mother of Henry's queen Elizabeth of York. When news of events in Ireland reached England at the beginning of 1487, the King summoned the Council to Sheen Palace to discuss the situation and plan countermeasures. It was decided to offer forgiveness to everyone who had helped the pretender 'lest (they) should in despair of pardon have no alternative but to persist in their resolution'; to take the Earl of Warwick to St Pauls and other places where he could be seen by, and could speak with, any who thought the boy in Ireland was genuine; and to deprive Elizabeth (to quote Vergil) 'by the decree of the same council of all her possessions'.[20] Vergil says that she was punished because she had endangered Henry's cause by surrendering her daughters (including his intended bride Elizabeth) to Richard III in 1484; but Henry knew this when he restored her to her royal dignity after Bosworth, and the measures taken at Sheen show that he was concerned with the present conspiracy rather than with an 'offence' which had made no difference to him. His problem was that he could not accuse his mother-in-law of plotting against him, still less put her on trial, without proclaiming the weakness to his dynasty to the courts of Europe, and so pretended that the disloyalty which merited her punishment had predated his reign.

Elizabeth was confined in Bermondsey Abbey, where, in Lord Bacon's words, 'it was almost thought dangerous to visit her, or see her'.[21] Henry ensured that she had no access to money,[22] (a decision which may imply that her contribution to the scheme had been partly financial), and she passed the remaining five years of her life in virtual seclusion. She is perhaps an unlikely conspirator in the sense that 'success' would have resulted in the deposition of her daughter and son-in-law, but the situation at court may not have been much to her liking. The younger Elizabeth had not become Henry's confidant (his mother, Margaret Beaufort, would always fulfil this role), nor had she been crowned. The King was determined to show that his title owed nothing to his wife although many had supported him for this reason; and Elizabeth Woodville is said to have considered her daughter 'not advanced but depressed'.[23] She had feared the Duke of Clarence's ambitions and would have had no wish to deliver the crown to his son at the expense of her own child; but she may have hoped that Elizabeth of York would be married to Warwick after Henry and his insufferable mother had been vanquished. There is, of course, no evidence that she actively sought this outcome, but it would have restored her to the centre of politics while allowing her daughter to remain queen.[24]

The second individual to be punished for what we must assume was his involvement in the conspiracy was Robert Stillington, who had been Bishop of Bath and Wells since 1465. Stillington was a career civil servant who had served Edward IV as Keeper of the Privy Seal from 1461 to 1467 and then as Chancellor for much of the period between 1467 and 1473.[25] We do not know why Edward decided to replace him in 1473, but it may not be unconnected with his close association with the Duke of Clarence. He had apparently helped to persuade Clarence to return to the family fold before the battle of Barnet, and was arrested and sent to the Tower after the Duke's execution in February 1478. Edward's treatment of his brother has always been considered harsh and, to some extent, inexplicable; and Professor Kendall's suggestion that Stillington had told the Duke what he was later to tell Richard of Gloucester – that Edward's marriage to Elizabeth Woodville was invalid – may well be true. The charge against Stillington was that he had 'uttered words prejudicial to the King and his state', and he may have been required to swear a private oath not to repeat them before he was fined and pardoned in June.

Stillington kept his guilty secret for the rest of King Edward's lifetime, but in 1483 Duke Richard was able to use it to bastardise his brother's children and become king in his nephew, Edward V's place. He seems to have retired from public life after drafting the Act of Parliament which conferred the crown on Richard, but Henry Tudor still ordered his arrest the day after Bosworth. The King's agents brought him to York in great distress 'sore crased by reason of his trouble', and were persuaded by the mayor, Nicholas Lancaster, to allow

Initial letter from the Register of Robert Stillington, Bishop of Bath and Wells, showing a hunter, armed with a crossbow, aiming at a fantastical bird.

him to 'continue still within the said citie for iv. or v. days for his ease and rest'.[26] He pleaded 'his grete age, long infirmite and feblenes',[27] when he successfully petitioned for a pardon in November, and then made his way to Oxford where, we may suppose, he met Richard Simons and Lovel. There is no evidence that he recruited Simons or masterminded the conspiracy; but he probably knew Warwick (his friend Clarence's son) as well as anyone and helped groom Simnel for his role. Henry again ordered his arrest in March 1487, but he took refuge in the University and refused to surrender. The masters tried to protect him – they argued that they could not, in conscience, compel him to yield to the King's agents – but the threat of force and the loss of their franchises appears to have changed their minds.[28] He was taken to Windsor where he was presumably interrogated and spent some time in confinement before ending his life in comparative obscurity. His commitment to Clarence and Clarence's son were central to his treasons, and the King undoubtedly 'thought him a dangerous man'.[29]

Elizabeth Woodville and Robert Stillington were unlikely bedfellows. She cannot other than have resented his part in the deposition of her son four years earlier, but the present, and the recovery of her former influence, was now more important than the past. The fact that Henry took action against them in February and March 1487 implies that he had already, to some extent, penetrated the conspiracy, but he seems to have had no inkling of the intentions of John de la Pole. The Earl of Lincoln had been appointed President of the Council of the North by his uncle King Richard (a decision which may imply that the childless monarch intended to name him his successor in preference to Warwick), and Henry Tudor's victory at Bosworth had severely damaged his prospects. He accompanied the new King on his 1486 progress and had apparently come to terms with the situation; but the loss of his great offices probably rankled and he was contacted by Lovel's followers when the royal party reached York. The rebels were dispersed shortly afterwards and Lincoln was probably relieved that he had not 'gone over the walls' to join them, but Simnel's backers would have done their utmost to draw him into their conspiracy in the latter half of the year. He was present at the meeting of the Council which deprived Elizabeth Woodville in February, but slipped away to Malines on 9 March (the same day that Henry ordered Stillington's apprehension), where he joined Duchess Margaret and Lovel.

Lincoln may have feared that the net was beginning to close on him also, but his departure was no spur of the moment decision. James Taite, a Tudor sympathiser, told the mayor and council of York that he had met several of the Earl's servants disguised as merchants at Doncaster on Lady Day (25 March). They were taking his horse and a quantity of gold and silver northwards, and intended to contact the Prior of Tynemouth and Sir Thomas Mauleverer. One of them boasted that 'John of Lincoln shall yeve theme all a breakfast that oweth hyme noo luff (love) nor favour', but confided that they had small hopes of winning over the Earl of Northumberland, 'he dothe both litill for us, therfor we sett litill by hyme'.[30] Lincoln was a high profile leader with the potential to attract others to him, but may have had his own agenda, known, perhaps only to Lovel and Duchess Margaret. Stillington and others were genuinely committed to Warwick, but it seems unlikely that a man who had been heir-presumptive would risk everything to gain the crown only to hand it to his young cousin. Some contemporaries thought that he meant to become king himself if the rebellion succeeded, and they were probably correct.

The conspiracy had not been without its difficulties, but the leading rebels were probably satisfied with their progress as they contemplated the approach of Easter. Elizabeth Woodville and Bishop Stillington had been eliminated, but Abbot Sante and his cell remained undetected (he had sent money to the Netherlands for Lincoln's use as early as January), while the others were beyond Henry's reach. The funds provided by Duchess Margaret and other sympathisers were used principally to hire shipping and a force of 1,500–2,000 German and Swiss mercenaries, *landsknechts*, professional infantrymen who had fought for Maximilian against rebels in the Low Countries and in his wars against the French. They were commanded by Martin Schwartz, a former Augsburg shoemaker, who had gained an invidious reputation for ruthlessness by allowing his men to burn and pillage the towns of Alost and Nineveh after recapturing them in 1485. Margaret had personally asked Maximilian to restrain him after Ghent surrendered, and it is possible that his employers were almost as relieved as the good townspeople when he took service with Lincoln and Lovel. We do not know precisely when the three of them left Burgundian territory and sailed for Ireland, but it cannot have been more than a few weeks after Lincoln's arrival. Lovel and Margaret would have known for some time that the Earl had been won over and his formal defection completed this stage of their plan.

A landsknecht *(sixteenth-century woodcut after David de Necker).*

Henry responded to Lincoln's flight to Malines by showing himself to the Duke of Suffolk's well-wishers in the course of a royal progress through East Anglia, and by ordering the detention of the Marquess of Dorset, Elizabeth Woodville's son by her first marriage, as he approached the royal party at Bury St Edmunds. There was every likelihood that the Earl would invade eastern England and try to gather support in his ancestral territories when the Irish rebels attacked the opposite side of the country, and the King sought to boost his popularity in the de la Pole heartland while neutralising those whose loyalty was not above suspicion. Dorset claimed that he wanted to see Henry 'to purge himself of some accusations which had been made against him',[31] but Henry was too cautious, or sceptical, to give him audience. Bacon says that the King 'kept an ear for him' (i.e, was prepared to give him a fair hearing on another occasion), but instructed the Earl of Oxford to take him to the Tower 'to preserve him from doing hurt either to the king's service or to himself'.[32] Henry supposedly remarked that 'if he were hys frende he should not be miscontented to suffre so lytle a reproche & rebuke for his princes pleasure',[33] and he accordingly played no part in the Simnel affair.

The King had decided that the forces he was assembling to counter the rebellion should rendezvous at Coventry (from where they could be despatched to whichever part of the country they were most needed), and accordingly took up his position there about 22 April. When he learned that his enemies had sailed for Ireland, and that there would be no immediate descent upon England, he allowed some of his men to return to their counties while he himself retired to Kenilworth castle to await developments. Lincoln's arrival in Dublin seems to have further emboldened the Irish nobles, and on 24 May Simnel was crowned 'King Edward VI' in Christchurch Cathedral (with a coronet borrowed from a statue of the Virgin since no crown was available), and shown to the people on the shoulders of Lord Darcy of Platten, the tallest man of his time. His supporters now included the Archbishop of Dublin, Walter Fitzsimons, a cluster of Irish lords, bishops and abbots, and, most significantly, Henry's deputy lieutenant in Ireland, Gerald 'Garret Mor' Fitzgerald, eighth Earl of Kildare.

Vergil tells us that it was Kildare's brother, Thomas, who had taken the lead in rallying support for Simnel in Ireland, but he could not have done so without the Lord Deputy's tacit approval. Kildare was a law unto himself in the sense that the country was virtually ungovernable without him, and Henry VII had perforce confirmed him in office notwithstanding his good service to Edward IV and Richard III. It is possible that he considered declaring himself independent of all English authority, but the cost of maintaining Schwartz's mercenaries would have been considerable and a policy which concentrated on

Christchurch Cathedral, Dublin.

defending Ireland against a Tudor re-conquest would have held little attraction for Lincoln and Lovel. He did not sail with the rebel army, evidence perhaps, of a certain caution or a less than total commitment to the enterprise; but he was happy for his brother to raise troops from among his royal master's subjects, principally 'kernes', lightly armed footmen. It is unlikely that he believed in the pretender (although some writers suggest he may have thought him genuine); but convinced or not, he is unlikely to have imparted his doubts to those he encouraged to invade England on the boy's behalf.

Ireland was also the destination of two other prominent Yorkists who joined the rebellion, the Cornish knight Sir Henry Bodrugan, and Richard Harliston, the former governor of Jersey. Bodrugan was a lawless and rumbustious individual who was pardoned on at least four occasions between 1467 and 1480 and also had to secure the reversal of an attainder imposed on him for failing to answer an indictment in 1474. He and his associates seem to have terrorised Cornwall, breaking and entering, engaging in piracy, extracting and misappropriating money under cover of the King's commission, and corrupting wills. Parliament was informed that

> 'it is openly known in the said shire that the said Henry Bodrugan, not doubting God, nor the dreadful censures of the Church ...

taketh upon him to prove testaments of the people there, both of people of great substance of goods and others, to change their last wills damnably, take yearly great sums of goods and also to commit the administration of like persons dying testate and intestate at his pleasure, and seizeth and taketh by colour thereof all goods and chattels of such persons so dying, and then to his own use taketh and converteth to the worst example that may be.'

His victims complained that they could obtain no common law remedy against him 'for if any person would sue the law against the said Henry . . . or against any of their servants, anon they should be murdered and slain and utterly robbed and despoiled of all their goods.'[34] He survived because, like many of his kind, he always had a faintly plausible answer to the charges brought against him, and because Edward IV and Richard III had little alternative but to use the services of a man who clearly had the 'rule' of his native shire.

Bodrugan tentatively maintained his position at the beginning of Henry VII's reign, but the King ordered his arrest when he moved against Elizabeth Woodville and Bishop Stillington. It was alleged that, together with his son, John Beaumont, and other rebels he had 'withdrawn into private places in the counties of Devon and Cornwall and stir up sedition', and he and Beaumont were attainted of high treason, charged with 'imagining and compassing the death of the King in company with the Earl of Lincoln' after they subsequently escaped to Ireland. His heirs later claimed that he had gone to Ireland to visit a kinsman and 'was never in company with the said Earl, nor never spake with him, nor never sent him message by writing, nor none otherwise, nor never committed treason';[35] but it would be unwise to trust the testimony of those who hoped to recover some of his forfeited properties. They also stated that he died there 'soon afterwards' and could not, therefore, have participated in the invasion; but claims that an individual had died *before* a lost battle were not unknown in medieval England,[36] and they clearly wanted to distance him from what had happened at Stoke.

Bodrugan was loyal in his rough and ready manner, but Richard Harliston, who was brought up in Richard, Duke of York's household and subsequently helped drive the French from Jersey, had a more distinguished record of service to the Duke's sons. He became a popular English governor, remembered for adding the tower which bears his name to Mont Orgueil castle, for helping to found the first school on the island, and for his custom of giving a coin to every boy he found practising archery. He attempted to hold the castle against Henry VII after Bosworth (a later chronicle claims that he planned to deliver it to Duchess Margaret), but he was dislodged and eventually pardoned in October 1486. It is uncertain whether he joined Lincoln in Burgundy or made his own way to Ireland, perhaps after being contacted in England by Lovel; but he was clearly unhappy with the state of the world and believed the verdict of Bosworth could still be changed.

Harliston's command on Jersey meant that, unlike most of his fellow conspirators, he was well versed in maritime matters, and he is likely to have been involved in assembling and equipping the rebel fleet – perhaps in the Netherlands or Ireland or in both countries – and in ensuring that it reached England safely. The ships were ready by the end of May, and the motley army, Schwartz's *landsknechts*, an unknown but substantial number of Irish commanded by Sir Thomas Geraldine, and the few Englishmen who had either accompanied Lincoln and Lovel or had joined them later, prepared to embark on their great enterprise. It is impossible to know how they rated their prospects; but their army was considerably larger that the force which had landed at Milford Haven with Henry Tudor two years earlier, and they clearly hoped that many former Neville and Ricardian supporters would join them when they reached England. They sailed out of Dublin and landed on the coast of Lancashire on 4 June 1487.

Chapter 3
National Politics and Local Rivalries

It is likely that many northerners – and not a few southerners – sympathised with the broad aims of the Simnel rebellion, but open commitment to it was another matter. The Act of Attainder passed against the leading rebels after the battle names twenty-eight individuals who either arrived with the invading force or joined it in England, but the list does not make very impressive reading. There was Lincoln, of course, together with Bodrugan, Beaumont and Harliston, and a squire and two gentlemen who had accompanied the Earl into temporary exile;[1] but apart from these only one knight, seven squires, ten gentlemen, and four yeomen were formally indicted. The knight was Sir Thomas Broughton, who had briefly sheltered Lovel in Lancashire after the failure of his 1486 uprising, and he was joined by his brother John and two other former rebels, the squires Richard Middleton and Edward Frank. There were two members of the extended Harrington family, Thomas, and Sir Robert's son, James; Robert Percy, whose father had fallen at Bosworth; four gentlemen named Mallary from Northamptonshire (Queen Elizabeth Woodville's ancestral county); and ten others including Roger Hartlington of Hartlington in Craven (Yorkshire) who had served King Richard as a yeoman of the Crown. They were predominantly northerners – relatively few southerners would have been able to join an army which penetrated only a short distance into southern England – and (with the possible exception of Broughton) had little to contribute besides themselves.

Francis Lovel was not attainted in 1487 because he had been included in the Act passed against Richard III's principal supporters two years earlier, and the same may be true of Sir Robert Harrington and Sir Thomas Pilkington. These last two had been pardoned in September 1486 and their lands and goods restored to them 'as if (their) blood had never been corrupted by attainder';[2] but their estates were given to Lord Stanley (now Earl of Derby) in September 1489. They had, presumably, forfeited their pardons by joining the Simnel rebellion, and there was no need to ask Parliament to indict them because their original convictions had never been reversed. The fact that it was Robert's son, James, who was formally deprived of his family's properties implies that his father had been killed in the battle, and nothing more is heard of Pilkington.

Sir James Harrington (Robert's brother) may also have been implicated, but this is less certain since his 1486 pardon did not specifically include the restoration of his properties. They were given to Sir Edward Stanley, and James was still living in poverty as late as 1497.[3]

There were also many who joined or supported the rebellion but who for various reasons escaped the supreme penalty. The Earl of Northumberland ordered Sir Robert Plumpton to arrest John Pullen of Scotton (Yorks.) and Richard Knaresborough, Richard III's bailiff of Leicester, a week after the battle,[4] and Thomas Metcalf of Nappa (Yorks.), who had received a pardon in November 1485, was fined 1,000 marks between August 1487 and January 1488.[5] The two Lords Scrope, John of Bolton and Thomas of Masham, who played (as we shall see), a somewhat equivocal part in the uprising, were obliged to find sureties for their future behaviour and to reside in southern castles after the battle; and a similar punishment was imposed on Sir Edmund Hastings of Roxby beside Pickering, who, Dr Cunningham suggests, may have been a member of their contingent.[6] King Henry wrote to Pope Innocent VIII to complain that Richard Redman, Abbot of Shap and Bishop of St Asaph, had assisted the rebels, but Redman's involvement did not prevent him from being translated to Exeter in 1496 and to Ely in 1501. They were all forgiven with the possible exception of Knaresborough, and pardons were granted to seventy-one other individuals between August 1487 and August 1489.[7] Most are little more than names in the record and it is impossible to assess their culpability; but the vast probability is that, in most cases, their offences related to the rebellion, and that at least some had fought at Stoke.

We have looked at those who joined the rebellion in some detail, but it is no less important to consider who did not. The fact that a comparatively large number of peers, knights and gentry rallied to Henry VII suggests that most politically aware Englishmen were not actively seeking a change of government,[8] and some former rebels (and potential supporters) undoubtedly sat 'on the fence'. A number of those who had resisted the King at the beginning of his reign did, as we have seen, continue to oppose him; but Sir Robert Middleton and Sir John Huddleston preferred to retain Henry's favour, and there is nothing to suggest that men like Geoffrey Frank, John Ward and Thomas Otter caused further trouble. Lincoln's attempt to recruit Sir Thomas Mauleverer apparently foundered (he was fined 100 marks and bound under £300 on 2 June, only two weeks before the battle),[9] and the bonds previously imposed on Sir Christopher Ward and several members of the Conyers family proved sufficient to ensure their loyalty. It is sometimes suggested that Sir Ralph Assheton of Ashton-under-Lyne (Lancs) joined the rebellion and was killed at Stoke but this is uncertain. Sir Ralph, a knight of the body to Richard

III, was a harsh landlord whose effigy was for many years paraded through Ashton on Easter Monday, and the alternative story, that he was murdered by a woman or died in a local uprising, may well be accurate.[10] All that is known is that he disappears from the record between 1487 and 1489.

This lukewarm reaction must have disappointed the rebel commanders and caused them to question some of their previous assumptions. They stood to lose everything – chattels, lands, even their lives, if the uprising faltered, and would not have challenged a reigning king in his own country unless they thought they had enough support to overthrow him and that the potential benefits outweighed the risks. The lesser men, including, probably, many of those pardoned without penalty, joined because they were committed or obligated to one or another of the leaders and were treated with appropriate leniency; but for Lincoln and Lovel, and for families like the Harringtons and Pilkingtons, the whole enterprise was an enormous gamble which spelled disaster if it failed to bring success.

It is often supposed that the leading rebels were motivated by their loyalty to the Yorkist cause in general, and to the House of Neville in particular; but closer examination of the evidence suggests that there were personal and local considerations which were equally important to them. There can be little doubt that the Earl of Lincoln hoped to become king if the insurrection succeeded and that, for him, the ultimate prize outweighed all other factors; but even he may not have been immune from concerns affecting his family's regional hegemony in East Anglia. The battle of Bosworth had destroyed the influence of the Howards, the de la Pole's great rivals, in the eastern counties (John, Duke of Norfolk, had been killed and his son Thomas, Earl of Surrey, imprisoned), but had restored the long-vanquished Earl of Oxford to his seat at Castle Hedingham in Essex. Lincoln's father, the Duke of Suffolk, would have to tread carefully if his close relationship to the Yorkist kings – and to Richard III in particular – was not to be held against him, and it was inevitable that Henry Tudor would prefer the claims of a man who had shared his exile and helped him to victory. Success at Stoke would have again removed Oxford without automatically restoring the Howards, and East Anglia would have become the fiefdom of the de la Poles.

Francis Lovel was among the late King Richard's most committed supporters, and perhaps needed no other reason to oppose his supplanter; but his presence in the rebel army helps to explain why at least one traditional 'Yorkist' chose to fight against it. William Hastings, Edward IV's friend and chamberlain, held lands which had once belonged to the extended Lovel family, and Francis laid claim to the Leicestershire manors of Ashby de la Zouch and Bagworth together with properties in Leicestershire and Lincolnshire forfeited by his uncle Viscount Beaumont, after Lord William's execution in June 1483. Lovel had no legal title to the lands in question – he had formally quitclaimed, or rescinded, his interest in Ashby (which his Zouch and Burnell ancestors had held of the Beaumonts) three years previously; Bagworth had been sold to the Hastings family by his father, Lord John Lovel; and William Beaumont (and his heirs and successors) had been deprived of their estates by Act of Parliament[11] – but such niceties could not restrain a man who was now among the greatest in the kingdom and was prepared to use violence to achieve his objectives. In 1481, for example, he sent his retainer Sir Robert Markham and other followers to 'make an entre' into the Bishop of Winchester's manor of East Bridgford, near Nottingham, which he claimed as co-heir to the entailed lands of William Deincourt, his grandmother's brother; and it is likely that violence was again imminent when the King intervened to defuse the 'traverse & variaunce' which had arisen between Lovel and his cousin, Henry, Lord Morley, for possession of the manor and lordship of Clayton, in Buckinghamshire, in December 1483.[12] Lady Katherine Hastings and her son Edward had good reason to fear Lovel's predatory ambitions, and the 'variaunce and grudge' as the deed calls it, was only partially assuaged on 5 May 1485 when, after the 'mediation of frendes', Lady Katherine agreed to give Lovel a cash payment of 200 marks and lands to the value of a third part of his uncle's estates not exceeding 200 marks per annum in return for the peaceful enjoyment of Ashby and Bagworth and the remainder of the Beaumont properties. But Francis was careful to emphasise that he had accepted the compromise because, in the words of the agreement, 'the said variances cannot finally be appeased during the nonage (minority) of the said Edward Ld Hastyngs': and it would appear that he meant to renew his claim when Edward came of age in November 1487.[13] The beleaguered King Richard was now actively 'planting' trusted supporters in diffident localities; and although assurances had been given to Lady Katherine it was unlikely that a close friend who was both the scion of an old Midlands family and the 'natural' successor to his uncle in Leicestershire and Lincolnshire would have had his ambitions in the region thwarted.[14] There can be little doubt that, had Richard lived, the Hastings family would have lost much of its authority in the eastern Midlands to the Lovels, and it is hardly surprising that in June 1487 the 'Yorkist' Edward Hastings fought for Henry Tudor – and against his arch-rival Francis Lovel – at the battle of Stoke.

Disputes over land, the greatest single measure of wealth, were commonplace in medieval society, and may explain why three, and possibly four, members of the Harrington family joined the rebellion.[15]. Their troubles began when Sir Thomas Harrington and his eldest son, Sir John, were killed fighting for the House of York at Wakefield in 1460. Sir James Harrington, Sir Thomas's second son, took possession of the family estates and he and his cousin Sir John Huddleston assumed custody of the infant heiresses, Sir John's daughters Ann and Elizabeth. Sir James proved his own worth to the Yorkist government by helping to capture Henry VI in 1465, but his success did not prevent the Stanleys, his rivals for influence in Lancashire, from casting covetous eyes on his recently acquired properties. Lord Thomas Stanley was distantly related to Ann and Elizabeth Harrington, and may have prompted the commissions of inquiry which found that Sir James had no right or title to the inheritance in 1468. Stanley became the girls' guardian, married them to his younger son Sir Edward and another relative, and framed a petition to the King in which they complained that their uncle had 'them kept as prisoners contrary to their wills, in divers places by long space, intending the utter destruction and disinheritance of the said complainants until the time they were by your high commandment delivered out of his keeping into the keeping of the Lord Stanley.' The Stanleys had clearly won the legal argument, but found they could not dislodge Sir James from Hornby Castle or the other manors which had belonged to his father and brother. A group of arbitrators headed by the Earl of Warwick failed to find a solution, and on 5 March 1471 Warwick's and Henry VI's government ordered a carriage to convey the cannon 'Mile Ende' from Bristol to Hornby to help Stanley besiege it. But when, nine days later, Edward IV returned to reclaim his kingdom, both James and Robert Harrington and Sir William Stanley, Lord Stanley's brother, all hurried to join him. Edward's bold gamble succeeded, but Lord Thomas would have been well placed to make his family's peace with Warwick and King Henry if it had failed.

The problem for King Edward – and for Richard III when he succeeded – was that both families were committed to his government after 1471. He could not favour one without offending the other, but royal intervention, or the appearance of it, was clearly necessary to preserve the peace. In 1473 the King asked Richard, Duke of Gloucester, the Harringtons' especial good lord, to resolve the matter, and with war with France looming a compromise was finally reached. Sir James was described as 'late of Hornby' when Edward pardoned all his offences three years later, but was given licence to crenellate the manors of Farleton and Brierley (where he had continued to reside throughout the 'troubles') in 1480. No further outbreaks of violence are recorded, and the agreement apparently held while the Yorkist kings reigned.

The protagonists kept the accord because it gave them part of what they wanted and because it was impolitic to be branded a troublemaker; but the situation changed dramatically in August 1485. Ian Grimble has suggested, probably correctly, that the Stanleys' decision to desert Richard III at the last moment at the battle of Bosworth owed something to their designs on the rest of the loyal Harringtons' properties, and helps to explain their uncharacteristically bold action. Lord Thomas and Sir William Stanley were richly rewarded by Henry Tudor, the beneficiary of their treachery, while James and Robert Harrington were attainted and their lands seized by the new ruler. The estates which had once belonged to their father and brother should now have passed to the surviving heiress Elizabeth; but she had remarried following the death of her Stanleyan husband and it now suited Lord Thomas and his brother to pretend that the male Harringtons had always been the rightful owners! So much for their protests at the depredations she had allegedly suffered at the hands of her uncles twenty years before!

It is also possible that the Stanleys' deceit did not end with Henry VII's victory. Sir James Harrington had an only (illegitimate) son, John, who he made his heir shortly before he left to join Richard of Gloucester's Scottish campaign in 1481. John died in mysterious circumstances at an unknown date (it may have been a little before, but was more probably a little after, the battle of Bosworth), and Elizabeth Harrington wrote to her second husband expressing the belief that he had been poisoned by her former brother-in-law Sir Edward Stanley. Sir Edward had been granted Sir James's estates, of course, and Elizabeth suspected that he had had the young man eliminated to prevent him from seeking the reversal of his father's attainder and the restoration of at least some of his properties. The Stanleys' victory was total, and the Harringtons' only real hope of countering it lay in removing the king their rivals had created. They may not have supported Lincoln, still less have believed in Simnel; but the rebellion presented them with an opportunity to turn the tables on their local rivals and they seized it with both hands.

The Harringtons faced a bleak future, and the same sense of hopelessness may have persuaded Richard Harliston, the former governor of Jersey, to join the rebellion. Henry Tudor had found sanctuary in Brittany following his escape from England in the aftermath of Edward IV's victory at Tewkesbury, and C.S.L. Davies has suggested that Harliston may have been involved in the negotiations by which Richard III persuaded Pierre Landais, the Breton treasurer, to return him to England in 1484.[16] Henry's friends learned of the agreement, and he was spirited across the French border hours before Landais's men arrived to arrest him; but it had been no thanks to Harliston the scheme had faltered and he was presumably thereafter a marked man. This may be why he tried to prevent Jersey from falling into Henry's hands after the battle of Bosworth, and it is not without interest that the King ordered Edmund Weston, a former comrade, to besiege him in Mont Orgueil castle.

Weston had married a Jersey girl and settled on the island after helping Harliston recapture it from the Lancastrians in 1468, and although he had not shared Henry's exile the grants appointing him governor of Guernsey stressed his 'good and gratuitous services' and the financial sacrifices he had made for the Tudor party.[17] Mathew Baker, whom Henry appointed joint governor of Jersey and Mont Orgueil in February 1486, was one of the friends who had fled with him across the Franco-Breton border, and Harliston could not hope to prevail against such well-connected rivals. His October 1486 pardon must have seemed small recompense for what he had lost on the island which had been his home for almost two decades, and, like the Harringtons, his only hope of recovery lay in removing these acolytes of the new King.

Sir Henry Bodrugan's sharp practices must have made him many local enemies in the West Country, but there was one conflict in particular which was destined to spoil his relationship with Henry VII. He had loyally supported Richard III in what is known as 'Buckingham's Rebellion' in the autumn of 1483, and had been ordered to arrest his fellow Cornishman Richard Edgecombe, who had joined the uprising. There is a tradition in the Edgecombe family that Richard was driven to hide in thick woods at Cotehele overlooking the gorge of the Tamar,

> 'which extremity taught him a sudden policy, to put a stone in his cap and tumble the same into the water, while these rangers were fast on their heels, who looking down after the noise and seeing his cap swimming thereon, supposed that he had desperately drowned himself, gave over their further hunting and left him liberty to shift away and ship over into Brittany.'[18]

Richard became one of the principal servants of Henry Tudor's government after Bosworth, and must have felt a certain satisfaction when he was instructed to arrest Bodrugan in February 1487. Sir Henry was not caught unawares, however. He is said to have slipped from his house, made his way to the nearby cliffs, and 'leaped down into the sea upon a little grassy island there without much hurt or damage' from where a boat he had prepared for the purpose collected him and conveyed him to safety. These stories may be no more than local traditions, but there can be no doubt that Bodrugan (like Harliston and the Harringtons) would have smarted at the favour being shown to his local rival. His gamble failed, of course, and Edgecombe was granted most of his manors on 26 April 1488.

The fears which persuaded these men to seek to reverse the verdict of Bosworth were not confined to England. Gerald Fitzgerald, Earl of Kildare, had held sway in Ireland under the nominal authority of a succession of English governors, but may have felt his pre-eminence threatened by the revival in the fortunes of his principal local rival, Thomas Butler, Earl of Ormond. The Butler family represented the Lancastrian opposition to the Yorkist Fitzgeralds in Ireland, and had spent many years in the political wilderness for their loyalty to the deposed dynasty. Thomas's eldest brother, James, Earl of Ormond and Wiltshire, had been attainted and executed by Edward IV's government in 1461, and Thomas himself had fought for Henry VI and Queen Margaret at Tewkesbury ten years later. He was pardoned three months after the battle, however – perhaps, like other diehard Lancastrians, he recognised the futility of further resistance – and slowly began to recover royal favour. Some of his estates were restored to him and he was created a knight of the Bath at Richard III's coronation; but it was Henry VII who finally reversed the attainder, made him a privy councillor, and appointed him chamberlain to Queen Elizabeth of York. Men who had sacrificed much for Lancaster could expect to be preferred and rewarded by the new Lancastrian–Tudor monarch, and although Henry had been obliged by necessity to confirm Kildare in office in the short term, there could be little doubt it was Butler who enjoyed his confidence. The reality, of course, was that Kildare was too powerful and influential to be dismissed even after the rebellion, and Butler's new appointments necessitated his presence in England. But it is significant that a number of people with links to the Butlers – Nicholas St Lawrence (later Lord Howth) and the leading citizens of Waterford – all refused to recognise Simnel, and Kildare may have thought he saw the writing on the wall.

There were also others, including some associated with the Nevilles by marriage or long service, who, if they did not feel under threat in their traditional heartlands, would have shared Archbishop Rotherham's sentiments when Lord Hastings's messenger brought him word of the death of King Edward, that 'be it as well as it will, it will never be so well as we have seen it'.[19] Two rebels who may have been influenced by such considerations (and about whom we have some detailed, personal, information) are the two Lords Scrope, John of Bolton and Thomas of Masham. Lord John was a lifelong Yorkist who had fought at Northampton and been 'sore wounded' at Towton in 1461. Originally a Percy retainer, he had gravitated towards Richard, Duke of Gloucester (the future Richard III) in the 1470s, and, in the aftermath of 'Buckingham's Rebellion', had become Richard's principal agent in south-west England. He was rewarded with lands in Somerset, Devon and Cornwall worth £206 11s. 8d., was appointed constable and steward of Exeter Castle at a salary of 200 marks together with an annuity of £126 18s. 4d. 'unto the tyme he be promoted' and was given the 'guyding and oversighte' of estates forfeited by John, Lord Welles, and the Bishop of Exeter.[20] But he could expect to retain little, if any, of this new-found wealth and influence under Henry, and had no reason to support him against a Yorkist challenger. The same is probably true of Lord Thomas, who joined him in his attack on York. Thomas was much younger, having come of age as recently as 1480; but he had married Elizabeth, the second daughter of John Neville, Marquess Montagu, and doubtless hoped for preferment if the young Earl of Warwick (his wife's second cousin) became king. They may, of course, have been moved by other considerations now lost to us, but the vast probability is that they had weighed the risks together, and, like the others, had decided that the opportunity was not to be missed.

These, then, were some of the connections, fears, and ambitions which Lincoln and the other promoters of the rebellion doubtless played upon in the weeks and months preceding the invasion. Not all those who were disaffected would have been willing to join them, and some of those who initially promised support would have prevaricated. It is likely that not a few paused to assess the rebels' chances of success before finally committing themselves (or alternatively, found an excuse to avoid direct involvement), and there was little to prevent even apparently firm friends from abandoning the enterprise if it appeared to falter. Lincoln, and particularly Lovel, could only hope that they had done enough.

Chapter 4

Alarums and Excursions

The enforced period of waiting, an oasis of calm before the coming storm, gave Henry an opportunity to relax at Kenilworth with his family while continuing to prepare to defend his kingdom. Towards the end of April he instructed Sir Richard Tunstall and six other northern knights to be ready to aid York if it was attacked by the rebels, and ordered the constable of Scarborough Castle to send the citizens twelve serpentines (light cannon), 'som mor some lesse, of diverse sortes, garnysshed with chambre and powder therunto'.[1] On 4 May he wrote to the Archbishop of York requesting that the Pope's bull threatening those who impugned his royal title with excommunication be promulgated at Furness Abbey and Cartmel Priory in north-west Lancashire (clear evidence that he expected trouble from that area); and on 3 June issued a proclamation ordering that spreaders of rumours 'untrue and forged tales and tidings' be set in the pillory.[2] Victuallers were warned to ensure that they had sufficient stocks of bread, ale, and horse-fodder 'at reasonable price in ready money' to sustain his army as he moved northwards, and anyone who took advantage of the situation to rob churches, rape women or settle quarrels was threatened with death.[3] The success of these measures is difficult to quantify. There is no evidence that Furness Abbey subsequently assisted the rebels and Henry does not seem to have suffered from a lack of provisions; but one of the knights he had ordered to help defend York, Sir Edmund Hastings, probably joined the two Lords Scrope in attacking it, and the constable of Scarborough Castle was unable to send any ordnance because he could not spare the only four cannon he had.[4]

There is no record of precisely where the rebels landed in England. The suggestion that it was on Piel Island seems rather improbable, and somewhere on the Furness peninsula is distinctly more likely. Sir Thomas Broughton, who was influential in the region, would doubtless have been among the first to welcome them, and tradition has it that they spent their first night on English soil camped on Swarthmoor, near Ulverston, which may or may not have been so named after Martin Schwartz. They were well-equipped – one source mentions that they had 'swerdys, speris, marespikes, bowes, gonnes, harneys brigandynes, hawberkes, and many other wepyns and harneys defensible',[5] and

next morning (Tuesday 5 June) began their long march to York. Their route would have taken them via Newby Bridge, Kendal, and Sedbergh into friendly Wensleydale, where they passed by or through Hawes, Castle Bolton and Middleham before reaching Masham on 8 June.[6] They had probably rested the previous night at Jervaulx Abbey (the abbot, William Heslyngton, had to seek a pardon after the battle), and found the dale a welcome respite after the rigours of the inhospitable fells.

Gold signet ring found in the castle with an impression of the seal. The date was probably (14)87.

Their hope was that local men who had previously adhered to Warwick 'the Kingmaker' and Richard of Gloucester would join them in substantial numbers, but few apparently did so. The gentry may have had enough of 'adventures in shining armour' (to quote G.M. Trevelyan),[7] and perhaps feared rather than welcomed the large contingents of 'foreigners' in Simnel's army. Lincoln, Lovel and their friends would normally have drawn the core of their support from their own 'connections' – men-at-arms from their household retinues and tenants (billmen and bowmen) from their properties – but Lincoln's estates lay in East Anglia and the Thames Valley, and Lovel, attainted in 1485, was effectively landless. They could only hope that old loyalties or the chance to steal a lead on local rivals would persuade some to support them, and may even have doubted the commitment of knights like Sir Robert Harrington and Sir Thomas Pilkington who had only recently made their peace with King Henry. The author of *The Great Chronicle of London* reports that Martin Schwartz confronted the Earl of Lincoln and accused him of self-deception,

> 'ffor when he took this voyage upon hym he was comffortid & promysid by therle of lyncoln, That grete strength of this land aftyr theyr landyng wold have Resortid unto the said Erle, But when he was fferre [far] entrid and sawe noo such Resort, Then he knewe well he was dyssayvyd [deceived], wherffor he said unto therle, sir now

see I well that ye have dyssayvyd your sylf & alsoo me, But that notwythstandyng, all such promyse as I made unto my lady the duchesse [Margaret], I shall perfform.'[8]

His criticism was unfair inasmuch as Lincoln and Lovel had already amassed a larger army than that which had fought for Henry Tudor at Bosworth, and had done their best to rally support in England in advance of their arrival. The depositions of Edward II, Richard II and Henry VI had only been effected after long periods of royal mismanagement, and many people who mattered politically would still have given Henry VII the benefit of the doubt in 1487. Even Edward IV had been greeted with caution, rather than enthusiasm, when he returned from exile in Burgundy, and it may have been the difficulty of finding a common language, or poor translation, which led Schwartz to believe that he had been promised more than he had.

It was from Masham that 'Edward VI' (as Simnel was now styled) despatched a letter to

'our trusty and welbiloved the maiour and his brethren and comunaltye of our citie of York' expressing the hope that 'ye woll show unto us your good aides and favourez, and where we and such power as we have broght with us by meane of travayle of the see and upon the land beene gretely weryed and laboured, it woll like you that we may have relief and ease of logeing and vitailles within oure citie ther.'[9]

Lincoln and Lovel were both well-known in York and hoped for a favourable reception; but the mayor and aldermen had for weeks past protested their loyalty to King Henry and had been busy strengthening their defences.[10] The city fathers knew that Tudor forces under the Earl of Northumberland and Henry, Lord Clifford were approaching, and they rejected the rebels' overtures with the grim warning that the citizens would 'withstand them with their bodies' if they attempted to gain access by force.[11] They may also have calculated that Lincoln would not turn aside to attack a city – albeit an important one – while armies were mustering against him, and their stance was justified when their emissaries returned next day with word that he 'was departid over Brugh-brig (Boroughbridge) and soo streght suthward'[12] with the intention of striking quickly – and directly – against the King. Lord Clifford had meanwhile arrived in the city with a force of some 400 horse and foot-soldiers, and on 10 June (Trinity Sunday) he set off in pursuit of the enemy, who that evening had bivouacked on Bramham Moor. Clifford's troops lodged at nearby Tadcaster, too close to the rebels for safety, and during the night part of

Lincoln's army fell upon them and sent them fleeing back to York in panic. The equipment and monies they had brought with them fell into the hands of the Yorkists, whose flagging spirits must have been lifted by this first 'victory' on English soil.

King Henry had stationed horsemen along the western coast of England to gather information about the rebels' preparations from travellers arriving from Ireland and to bring him word as soon as they appeared in person. It would have taken the most stalwart horseman between three and four days to cover the near 200 miles from Furness to Kenilworth where the King was staying, and it may have been late on Thursday or early on Friday (by which time his enemies were at Jervaulx or Masham) before word of the landing reached him. Polydore Vergil says that Christopher Urswick, Henry's chaplain and confessor, a native of Furness, was sent to the region to report on the depth and defensibility of the harbours; and that as he was returning to court he was overtaken by a courier bearing news of the rebels' landing and 'sent ahead a messenger to tell the king of the approach of his enemies and, following on the heels of the messenger, himself gave a fuller account of the whole matter.'[13] Henry at once ordered his friends to gather their forces, and moving north-east via Coventry reached Leicester on Trinity Sunday. His thoughts must have turned to his late adversary, King Richard, whose body was buried in the Grey Friars church and who had spent a night in the town before marching to defeat at Bosworth two years earlier. Henry, too, was leaving on the morrow to face an uncertain future, and his fears would have been multiplied had he known that Lord Clifford's forces were being routed near Tadcaster, quite literally as he slept. His rest may also have been disturbed by the carousing of the camp-followers who seem to have attached themselves to his army during its enforced period of inactivity. These 'harlatts and vagabonds' (as the herald who accompanied the Tudor forces described them) were unlikely to obey the royal proclamation forbidding theft and quarrelling, and many soon found themselves in Leicester prison. More were rounded up when the army reached Loughborough on Monday, 'wherfor', says the same writer, 'ther was more reste in the King's hooste, and the better rule'.[14]

The royal forces crossed the Leicestershire–Nottinghamshire border on Tuesday, 12 June, moving slowly to allow as many supporters as possible to bring in their men. Henry now had with him the Earl of Oxford (who had borne the brunt of the fighting at Bosworth), his uncle Jasper, Duke of Bedford, the Earls of Devon and Shrewsbury, Viscount Lisle, five barons including Lord Hastings, and a growing number of knights and squires. The herald names twelve knights broadly from the south of England (and one northerner, Sir William Troutbeck of Chester) who were made bannerets for

Engraving of seal of Jasper Tudor, Duke of Bedford.

their good services either before or after the battle, and mentions four others who were appointed 'for ryders', Sir Edward Woodville, Sir Charles Somerset, Sir Richard Haute and Sir Richard Pole. He also identifies fifty-two squires and gentlemen who were knighted, and Polydore Vergil lists fifty-two other notables, many of them Midlanders, who were with Henry from the beginning of the campaign or joined him as he moved northwards.[15] Edward Hastings had not, so far as is known, indented with any of his late father's predominately Midlands-based retainers, but no fewer than twelve of them (out of a maximum of sixty-six who were still living) fought with him in the royal army.[16] The others may have pleaded age and infirmity or may simply have escaped mention in the various records, but none of them was sufficiently opposed to Henry Tudor to support the rebels in 1487.

The battered Lord Clifford left York for the second time on Tuesday, 12 June (the same day the King crossed from Leicestershire into Nottinghamshire), this time in company with the Earl of Northumberland and a combined army of some 6,000 men. But when they were only a few miles from the city they were overtaken by a messenger bearing word that the two Lords Scrope 'constreyned as it was said by ther ffolkes' had attacked Bootham Bar in the name of King Edward and caused the 'comons being watchmen' to defend the gates.[17] It is unclear whether the assailants were acting in concert with Lincoln and Lovel or pursuing their own interests; but intentionally or not, they created a diversion which materially affected the Tudor's plans. The Earl of Northumberland immediately wrote to the mayor 'and desired hyme that he might come and entre the citie agane for diverse consideracions and causes hyme moveing'[18] and this meant that Sir Edward Woodville, who had brought

Bootham Bar, York, from Fragmenta Vetusta, or The Remains of Ancient Buildings in York, *by Joseph Halfpenny (1807).*

an advance guard of the royal army as far north as Doncaster (and who, presumably, intended to concert joint action with Northumberland) had to abandon his strategy and rejoin King Henry. The Burgundian chronicler Molinet says that Woodville (and possibly the other principal 'for ryders') retreated for three days through Sherwood Forest. They can hardly have rejoined the royal army later than Friday 15 June (the eve of the battle), and so probably abandoned Doncaster in the dying hours of the 12th after learning of Northumberland's intentions. The Yorkists were by this time within striking distance, and Woodville would have had little alternative but to run away.

Lincoln and Lovel had undoubtedly tried to persuade John and Thomas Scrope to join them as they passed through Wensleydale, but may have found them cautious, even reluctant, allies. Their attack on York may have been little more than a gesture designed (as the writer implies), to appease their tenants and well-wishers, and there is no evidence that they fought at Stoke. The same considerations may also explain why Northumberland chose to return to York when the citizens had already routed their assailants. Henry Percy had recovered the earldom, which his father had forfeited for his allegiance to Lancaster, in 1470, and had contrived to keep it by a deft mixture of loyalty and circumspection. When Edward IV returned from exile in 1471 Northumberland had declined to join him, but equally, had done nothing to impede his progress; and it was perhaps in much the same spirit that he had answered Richard III's summons to Bosworth fourteen years later but had played no part in the conflict.[19] He may have calculated that a policy of 'active neutrality' (i.e. appearing to do something while in fact doing nothing) would allow him to make his peace with both the King and the Earl of Lincoln according to circumstances; and it may have been for this reason that on Thursday, Corpus Christi Day, he and Clifford 'toke ther journey towardes the north parties'[20] and remained there until after the battle. Dr Goodman suggests that the Earl's intention was possibly to 'mop up Scrope's following';[21] but a responsible commander would not have deployed a large force against a scattered handful of local rebels when he was needed in another part of the kingdom unless, of course, it suited his purpose. Henry Percy must have known that his continued presence in northern England was unnecessary; but the Scropes' action had given him an excuse to march away from, rather than towards, the battlefield, and he was happy to accept it. He would be able to claim that he had remained loyal to the King in the event of a royalist victory, or to plead that he had withheld his support from Henry if the rebels triumphed. Both, he supposed, would choose to interpret his actions favourably, and he would emerge from the rebellion unscathed.

King Henry, meanwhile, passed Tuesday night 'in the felde, under a wood called Bonley Rice'[22] (Bunny) before approaching Nottingham next day. The herald reports that the royal harbingers had difficulty finding a suitable place for the army to bivouac on Wednesday, and the 'hooste wandrede her and ther a great espace of tyme' before the vanguard was ordered to take up a defensive position under a hill towards Nottingham. Henry found shelter in a 'gentilmannes place' at Ruddington, but the forces with him had to seek the hospitality of the villagers or settle for the colder comfort of a nearby bean field. Fortunately, the weather was 'marvelouse faire and wele tempered' (by English standards!), and if the ground was hard it was at least warm and dry.

We cannot gauge Henry's mood at this stage in his progress, but it was probably sombre. Many of the friends named by the herald and Polydore Vergil had by now joined him, and he expected a large force of Stanley retainers led by George, Lord Strange and Sir John Savage to arrive within the next twenty-four hours, but it was becoming apparent that others who had been summoned were playing a waiting game. Professor Mackie writes, 'if the evidence of *The Paston Letters* is not misleading there was some hesitation amongst the English gentry, men arguing as to the exact nature of the summons sent to them, and concerting joint action among themselves instead of answering at once the call of the king's lieutenant, Oxford'.[23] This uncertainty is unlikely to have been confined to East Anglia, and Lincoln and Lovel saw it as an opportunity to mount a campaign of disinformation which has no parallel in the conflicts of the period. They sent agents into various parts of England to spread alarm and despondency among potential recruits to the Tudor army, and although Henry's men captured several who 'noysede in the contrey that the King had ben fledde' (and hanged them from an ash tree on 'Notyngham Brygge ende' on Wednesday evening),[24] they could do little to counter other rumours 'by which subtyll meane & report many a trewe man to the kyng turnyd bak.'[25] Lord Bacon suggests that some royal 'supporters' were only too ready to believe stories which would excuse their absence from the coming conflict,[26] but there can be no doubt that others genuinely hesitated and one large contingent may even have fled. Molinet implies that, very late in the campaign, a large force which Lord Welles, the King's uncle, was bringing to his assistance 'turned like the others in flight' and fell back on London.[27] The Yorkists who were in sanctuary in the city assumed that Henry had been defeated and began to attack his supporters and cry for Warwick – clear evidence that the royal hold on the capital was tenuous and sensitive to changes in the political climate. Henry knew that Londoners would open their gates to a victorious Lincoln much as they had welcomed him after his triumph at Bosworth, and that some who had joined him from other parts of the country would support him only as long as he ruled England. Both rivals relied heavily on a relatively small group of committed followers, and both knew that only victory would secure the allegiance of the rest.

Thursday was a day of equally mixed fortunes. The King heard mass in Ruddington church, and then left his followers (without, apparently, explaining where he was going) to welcome Lord Strange and the Stanley contingent. He may have hoped that a period of uncertainty followed by relief and surprise when he returned with Strange's well-equipped forces would boost morale in the rest of the army; but it did not prevent a 'great skrye' (a commotion, or panic) from disturbing his camp in the evening 'whiche causede many cowards to flee.'[28] The herald does not tell us who, or what, was responsible for the trouble, but it is possible that word of Sir Edward Woodville's flight had raced ahead of his forces and sparked rumours that a vast rebel army was hard on his heels. The disorder was repeated the following night (Friday, the eve of the battle), perhaps this time in response to Sir Edward's less than happy reappearance, and must have caused Henry serious consternation. The writer makes light of the desertions, remarking that 'in this estrye (skyre) I harde of no man of worship that fledde but raskells';[29] but the fact remains that these were all people the King had supposed would fight for him in the coming battle. His situation was depressingly akin to that faced by Richard III before Bosworth, and the possibility that some of his friends were in touch with the enemy (and were prepared to behave as ambiguously as Northumberland to protect their interests against a Yorkist victory), can never have been far from his thoughts.

He need not have feared, however. The Stanleys' agenda left them with little alternative but to support the King they had created, and Lincoln and Lovel must have been devastated to learn that their attempt to reach the battlefield before Strange's contingent 'a great hoste, inow (enough) to have beten al the Kings enemies'[30] had failed by only thirty-six hours. We have no precise knowledge of the rebels' movements after they left the vicinity of Tadcaster on Monday until they passed by Southwell (some 14 miles north-east of Nottingham), on Friday, but an army which hoped to find supplies and add to its numbers would have chosen a route close to major centres of population. Lincoln and Lovel approached first Pontefract and then Doncaster from where the road through Bawtry (or Blyth), Retford and Tuxford would have brought them directly to Newark; but since the herald says that they 'passed by Southwell' it is more probable that they advanced via Tickhill and Worksop after leaving Doncaster before turning east towards the Trent at Mansfield.[31] We do not know where they rested or whether any of the towns opened their gates to them, but it is clear that they were still advancing as rapidly as possible.

Their march from Furness to Masham (a distance of at least 80 miles, much of it over rugged country) had been accomplished within four days of landing; and they had now covered the sixty-odd miles from Bramham Moor to Southwell, again in rather less than four days. Medieval armies encumbered with baggage and possibly cannon moved only slowly, and an average speed of over 17 miles daily was good progress by the standards of the period.[32] Like Henry, Lincoln and Lovel had given strict orders that there was to be no looting or damage inflicted (Vergil says they 'offered no harm to the local inhabitants')[33] in the hope that the populace would regard them as liberators rather than as a threat to life and property. But they were obliged to recognise that their army had probably already reached its maximum strength while the King's was still growing, and that everything depended on a swift and decisive stroke.

Henry's forward and personal divisions passed a second night south of Nottingham on Thursday while Lord Strange's forces rested some distance towards Lenton, and it was only on Friday that they marched eastwards to Radcliffe in response to news of the approach of the rebel army. Lincoln and Lovel may still have hoped to surprise the royal vanguard, but were probably aware that they were not alone in using agents and spies to hamper progress and report their enemies' whereabouts. Henry was too cunning a ruler not to have used every means available to him to counter the threat, and we need not doubt Edward Hall's comment that he 'was in hys (Lincoln's) bosome and knewe every houre what the Erle did.'[34] Curiously, perhaps, the whereabouts of the two armies immediately before the battle are less certain than when they were more distant. The herald says that on Saturday morning the King heard two masses conducted by Richard Fox, Bishop of Exeter, and that '5 good and true men of the village of Ratecliff (sic) whiche knew welle the countrey, and shewde wher wer marres and wher wer vilages or grovys for bushements (ambushes), or strayt weyes'[35] offered or were persuaded to conduct him towards Newark. The King gave two of these guides to Oxford, who advanced to Stoke, four miles south of Newark, where he encountered the enemy; and it was only towards the end of the fighting that Henry, who was some distance behind the vanguard, brought up additional forces from the south.

This is the 'standard' or generally accepted account of the royal army's movements immediately prior to the battle, but it conflicts with the sequence of events described by Polydore Vergil. Vergil thought that Henry had marched to Newark the day before the battle to deny the rebels access to the town, but could not prevent them from passing by him on the other side of the river. He then had no alternative but to retrace his footsteps southwards to engage them after they had crossed over and taken up battle stations near Stoke village, and

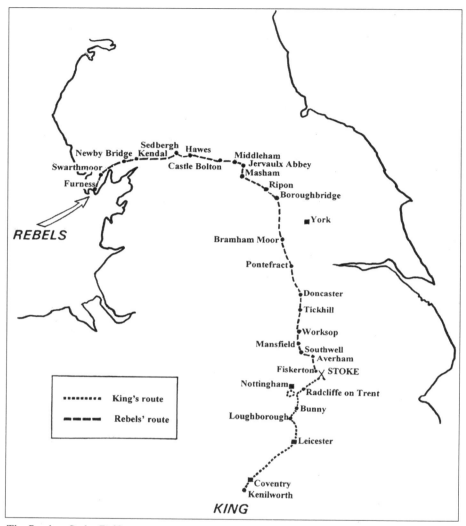

The Road to Stoke Field.

so approached from a northerly direction instead of from Radcliffe. Vergil was Henry's official historian and must have spoken to some who had taken part in the conflict; but he did not arrive in England until 1502 (or compose the first version of his work until 1512–13), and seems to have misunderstood what his informants told him. There can be no doubt that the herald, who was present, correctly reported the direction of the attack against the rebels; but it is possible to allow that Henry sent an advance guard to secure Newark and that these men rejoined the main army after it became apparent that they were no longer needed. Lincoln's men were probably hungry and would doubtless have appreciated some comfort; but he could not risk forcing entry into an unwilling town this close to his enemy any more than he had at York.

Molinet says that the rebels crossed the Trent at Newark, but this would have been difficult if, as Vergil suggests, it was held against them, and a waste of valuable time. The river divides into two arms north of Newark before again forming a single channel west of the town, and Lincoln would have been forced to cross both the western and eastern branches, the former at Kelham and the latter by the castle and the main centre of population. M.W. Bishop suggests that, alternatively, a passage may have been found near Farndon, between Newark and Stoke, and that the rebels then advanced the short distance along the Fosse Way to the battlefield;[36] but it is more probable that they left the Mansfield–Newark road at Averham and continued along the northern bank of the river via Staythorpe and Rolleston until they reached Fiskerton, the crossing point first suggested by R.P. Shilton, or Hazelford, further upstream. The river was narrower and shallower in 1487 than it is nowadays and could have been forded at either location;[37] but Fiskerton lies just to the north of the battlefield and is perhaps a more logical choice than Hazelford. Hazelford is closer to Burham Hill, the high ground which the rebels occupied, but its more southerly location would have taken them nearer to Henry and risked a surprise attack on their flank or rear. Here, probably on the afternoon of Friday, 15 June, Lincoln, Lovel, Schwartz, Sir Thomas Geraldine and others conferred to decide the exact deployment of their forces. Many months of planning, risk-taking and, more recently, hardship had brought them to these quiet fields in east Nottinghamshire where, in a few hours, their destinies and those of others would be decided. Now, they could only while away the short summer hours of darkness, and ponder what the morrow might bring.

Chapter 5

Trial by Combat

The reconstruction of a medieval battle is inevitably a tentative, cautious process. In the case of Stoke Field, the surviving printed sources and chance archaeological discoveries tell us only part of the story, and some writers have suggested that there is little merit in producing a version which is partly speculative and possibly inaccurate. John Gillingham's comment that 'many such maps [of the battle of Bosworth] have been drawn but, apart from the fun of making them, they are all quite worthless'[1] is still mentioned approvingly, although those who quote him and then go on to write about the battle invariably produce maps of their own! Dr Michael K. Jones has argued that it is virtually impossible to determine the course of events in a medieval conflict and express them diagrammatically. 'By piecing together a number of accounts, each from its own perspective, we can recapture some of the key moments and gather a sense of what took place (but) the order in which they took place, and the cause and effect between them, is ultimately unknowable'. The terrain, strategy and tactics are, he says, relevant 'if available evidence allows them to be determined'; but it is more profitable to consider the intangible, the motivation and mindset of the principal combatants. 'A surer sense of battle is to be found by focusing on why men fought' rather than by drawing neat maps which can never adequately express the chaos of the mêlée.[2]

It is, of course, entirely reasonable to examine, and indeed speculate upon, the wider, psychological aspects of a battle, but difficult to see how the thoughts of the soldiers (which are ultimately unknowable) can replace the verifiable reality of the landscape and the ways in which an army could, or could not, be deployed within it. The key to understanding a battle is surely to be found not in Jones's 'intangible' but in a scientific and methodical approach to the surviving evidence, one which seeks to reconstruct the historic terrain and is based on a full archaeological survey, a careful examination and concordance of the surviving literary sources, and a knowledge of the military practices of the period. It should be possible to use both documentary evidence and soil sampling techniques to determine areas of cultivation, marsh, woodland and the courses of roads and the river in the late-medieval era, and systematic fieldwalking by volunteers armed with metal detectors could lead to discoveries which would tell us much more about precisely where and how the battle was fought.[3] This would require permission from landowners, the engagement of specialists in soils analysis and the reconstruction of medieval field systems, and the establishment of a small but dedicated team of metal-detector users, all of which are unfortunately beyond the scope of the present survey. A funded study, possibly of several years' duration, would be needed to undertake a thorough and detailed investigation of this nature; but in the meantime we can still make full use of the literary sources, the widely used manual of the Roman military author Vegetius, and whatever details of the medieval landscape and archaeological discoveries are available to us. This is not ideal or perfect – few things are nowadays – but it is a better methodology than taking a modern map of the battlefield and positioning the armies upon it in a more or less arbitrary manner. We will inevitably have recourse to Colonel Alfred Burne's much-criticised principle of 'Inherent Military Probability', but our deductions will be as reasoned and reliable as the evidence permits.

We left the royal army at Radcliffe preparing to undertake the remaining few miles of their journey to the battlefield, where Oxford's vanguard arrived, according to the herald, some time before '9 of the clok'.[4] All commentators agree that Oxford's division bore the brunt of the fighting, the King's centre and rear wards being either largely uncommitted or entirely absent, and this begs the question of how and why the Earl engaged his enemies with the equivalent of one hand tied behind his back. It is, of course, likely that, as at Bosworth, Henry committed the bulk and the best of his troops to the foreward, but whereas the second division usually followed closely behind the van ready to provide support as necessary, Oxford seems to have found himself for the most part isolated at Stoke. The answer may lie in the fact that there were two routes to the battlefield, the well-known Fosse Way and an older, more direct, road, sometimes called the 'Upper Fosse', which ran from the Roman fort of Margidunum (Nottingham) through East Bridgford and Kneeton to the bridging station at Ad Pontem, just north of Stoke village. Both were probably partly overgrown and pitted (hence the herald's comment that the guides were needed to avoid unsafe ground and possible ambushes), and Henry may have ordered Oxford to advance along the Upper Fosse while his own division (and presumably the rearguard) marched eastwards along the road towards Grantham for a short distance before turning north-eastwards onto the Fosse Way proper. He probably assumed that Lincoln and Lovel, like Harold at Hastings, would choose to fight a defensive battle, and that Oxford would be able to halt within sight of the enemy and wait for the rest of the royal army to arrive and deploy on his right flank. The rebel attack forced Oxford to

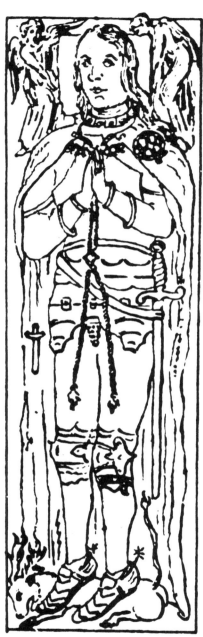

Drawing by Daniel King (1653) of tomb effigy of John de Vere, Earl of Oxford, destroyed in 1730.

defend himself, however, and by the time Henry's centre and rear wards reached the battlefield the victory had been all but won.

It may seem improbable that Henry would have divided his forces and risked part of them coming under attack without the support of the others, but the Fosse Way and Upper Fosse converge as they near Stoke, and the royal centre and rearguard would have found it easier to encircle the rebels if they had approached the battlefield from a little to the east of Oxford's division rather than immediately behind it. There would have been no need for Henry to retain the services of three of the five local guides if he intended merely to follow in Oxford's footsteps (this itself implies that he had decided to march parallel with, rather than to the rear of, the vanguard), and there would have been no difficulty if both halves of the army had reached their destinations more or less simultaneously. Oxford seems to have made good progress along the Upper Fosse and was in position within a few hours of breaking camp at Radcliffe, but the King had further to go with less-disciplined soldiers. He may have found the Fosse Way a more difficult passage than he had anticipated, and could only curse as his troops struggled along the long-neglected roadway. Scurriers would have brought him word that the battle was already in progress as the morning hours lengthened and he may have sent some mounted reinforcements on ahead or across country, but the majority of his forces were destined to play no part in the fight.

We might suppose that our documentary sources would tell us where – if not precisely how – the battle was fought, but this is by no means a foregone conclusion. Recent debate surrounding the battle of Bosworth has shown that nothing can be taken for granted,[5] and the clues provided by the chroniclers need to be examined very carefully. The Act of Attainder passed against Lincoln and his principal associates states that the rebels 'passed fro thens from place to place, to (till) they come to Stoke in the Countie of Notyngham', and may be the source of *The Great Chronicle of London*'s comment that they 'soo held on theyr Journay tyll they cam nere unto the fforesaid toun or vyllage of stook where they were encountrid wyth the kyngys hoost.' *The Book of Howth* agrees that 'both the armies came within a little to Stocke, and the morrow after joined and fought', while the York House Books' report that the rivals clashed on 'the more beyond Newark' was designed to convey the same information to local people, who would have been familiar with a major crossing point on the route southwards but who would not have heard of a small village in Nottinghamshire.[6] Two writers give actual distances. Molinet says that 'King Edward' 'came to Newark (and) marched through the country around two or three leagues' (5.6–8.4 miles) where he found the royal army 'at the end of a meadow near a village named Stoke', while the herald notes that the King 'reconnoitred his enemies and rebels ... beside a village called Stoke, *a large mile* out of Newark'[7] (my italics). This was not a statute mile of 1,760 yards or 1.61 km (an Elizabethan invention), but possibly a Roman mile (equal to a thousand paces or about 1.48 km), a country or 'long' mile (approximately double the length of a statute mile), or what R.P. Shilton calls a *computed* mile, 'generally found to be a statute mile and a half'.[8] Whichever is meant makes little difference, since they all fall as short of the actual distance between Stoke and Newark (four statute miles) as Molinet's estimate exceeds it. But the fact that they all relate the battle to Stoke (and not to any of the surrounding villages) means that there is no need to look outside the area for an alternative site.[9]

East Stoke is today a small settlement clustered around the area where the Fosse Way and the Upper Fosse adjoin Church Lane. The ground rises to a height of 57 metres above sea level four-fifths of a mile to the south-west of the village, and is known as the 'Burham Furlong' or 'Burham Hill'. This falls away gently to the east, forming a ridge extending across the Fosse Way and into the fields around Elston, but the western and north-western slopes descend more steeply to the flood plain of the Trent. A ravine or gully known as the 'Red Gutter' bisects the northern end of the escarpment, and emerges from the hanger called Stoke Wood near the modern road to the riverbank opposite Fiskerton. The ridge-top is an area of arable cultivation which in

R.P. Shilton's time boasted two windmills – one on either side of the Fosse Way – and is consistent with both the 'moor' of the York House Books and with Molinet's 'meadow'.

So far, so good, but the battlefield we see today has changed considerably since it was viewed by King Henry and the Earl of Lincoln in 1487. Stoke village was then considerably larger, extending along both sides of Church Lane as far as St Oswald's church, and Lincoln would have observed that the crofts and ancient enclosures around the farmhouses threatened to obstruct his main line of retreat in the direction of Newark. South of the village the meadows and fields were open, and this, together with the dry conditions, would have allowed both armies to deploy without undue difficulty. The present field system and the hedgerows are the result of enclosures made around 1800, and little or nothing remains of the ridge and furrow of the medieval furlongs to indicate which areas were grassland and which might have been avoided because they were ploughed and harder to negotiate. Even the Upper Fosse, which must have been a substantial track when, as we suppose, the King's army used it, has disappeared over the centuries, and only a small section (called Humber Lane) survives near the approaches to the village today.[10]

The precise extent of the ground occupied by each army would have been determined by these logistical considerations and by the number of troops at each commander's disposal. Estimates of the strength of the royal army range from the 10,000 of the York House Books (a figure which the author then spoils by claiming that the rebels numbered 20,000) to Molinet's absurd 50,000, and we have to rely mainly on Lord Bacon's comment that 'at least' 6,000 fighting men were added to the royal host by Lords Shrewsbury, Strange, and some 70 knights and gentlemen 'besides the forces that were with the king before'.[11] All recent commentators assume that Henry's overall strength was about 15,000 and that perhaps 6,000 of these were committed to Oxford in the vanguard,[12] a figure which bears out the general thrust of the information given to the York scribe (presumably by the 'servaunt of Master Recordour' who rode to the city immediately after the battle), that the Earl found himself significantly out-numbered. The Act of Parliament passed against the leading rebels says that Lincoln and Lovel had 8,000 men at their disposal, and this is broadly in keeping with what we can glean from other sources. Molinet, the Burgundian court historiographer, knew that Duchess Margaret had hired some 1,500–1,600 European mercenaries, the author of the Irish *Book of Howth* estimated that about 4,000 of his countrymen were lost in the enterprise, and however 'few' Englishmen had joined the army, they may still have numbered between two and three thousand. This is a higher figure than suggested by some writers, but Lincoln and Lovel, who knew of, even if they had not witnessed, the great hosts recruited in the 1460s and 1470s, would still have thought it disappointingly small.[13]

The rebels roused themselves at first light, partook of what little food they had with them, and then presumably heard mass. Richard Simons is the only priest known to have been present, but there were doubtless others, including, perhaps, several who were subsequently pardoned, who gave spiritual consolation to those about to hazard their lives in battle. Their prayers ended, they formed up and stood to order on Burham Hill and across the ridge ('on the brow of a hill' as André has it), and waited for Oxford to arrive and deploy his men 'on the level ground' a quarter of a mile to the south of his enemies' position in the vicinity of Trent Lane.[14] Vegetius estimated that each foot-soldier occupied a width of 3 feet when standing at order, so if Lincoln's forces stood six deep in a single body his line would have extended for a minimum of 4,000 feet, or three-quarters of a mile, across the Fosse Way and a short distance into Elston fields[15] (see Map 2). Oxford's smaller front, 3,000 feet long, would have stopped short of the Fosse (assuming that his left wing was positioned directly opposite the right of the rebel army), an entirely satisfactory arrangement if, as we suppose, he expected King Henry to march up the road to reinforce him and deploy additional forces on his right flank. There was the danger that his enemies would overlap him on the right if Henry failed to arrive promptly, and so he positioned 2,000 'horse' (almost certainly mounted men-at-arms and archers), commanded by Sir Edward Woodville on this side of his army to prevent his line from being 'turned' or attacked from behind. Molinet's figure may be exaggerated and he does not say that the decision was made for this reason, but Oxford clearly felt that greater strength was needed in this area than on his left wing where, according to the same writer, only 1,200 men were alloted to Sir John Savage.[16] It is likely that the royalists had many more horsemen than their opponents, but most would have dismounted and fought as infantry. Horses were useful for achieving surprise or pursuing a fleeing enemy, but the battle of Stoke, like other conflicts of the period, would have been fought largely in the 'English manner', on foot.

Within the armies soldiers would be divided into contingents recruited by particular noblemen or towns (or perhaps more according to nationalities in the case of the Yorkists), and then further sub-divided into companies of perhaps 100 gathered around a standard. Some writers argue for a fairly low level of organisation in Wars of the Roses armies, with men grouped according to lords or localities but in a rather vague or unstructured manner. This is possible – organisation must always have been better on some occasions than others – but it would have been difficult for a commander to issue all but the most general

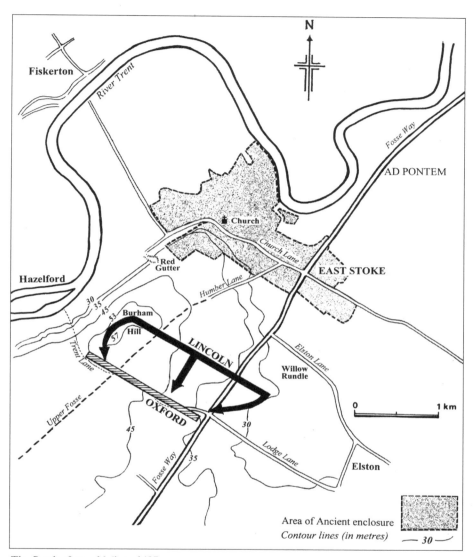

The Battle, 9 am, 16 June 1487.

of orders or even to calculate whether a particular piece of ground offered sufficient frontage for his army unless there was discipline, and order, among the ranks. 'Battle was undoubtedly chaotic, but military practice was designed to overcome that force of chaos. Indeed the central focus of offensive action was to break the coherence of the enemy deployment and to release the inherent chaos, for then the enemy became a vulnerable target and the "execution" could begin.'[17] Oxford's force was undoubtedly well-drilled and included some of the men who had fought with him at Bosworth. The professional mercenaries in the rebel army were perhaps even tougher; but the Irishmen, although brave to the point of recklessness, would have been more loosely organised and were more used to confronting opponents armed with similar weapons in their own land.

Numbers and organisation were only part of the equation, however. Equally important was the experience of the leaders and the quality and equipment of the men who fought under them. Few lords who had held positions of command in earlier Wars of the Roses battles were still active in 1487, and Henry was fortunate that his army was led by veteran warriors of the calibre of the Earl of Oxford and Sir Edward Woodville. His younger noble supporters, Strange, Shrewsbury and Hastings, were all sons of retired or deceased generals, but had virtually no experience of combat. The same was true of Lincoln and Lovel, who had not even been born when the Wars started, and who may or may not have been present at Bosworth. Lovel had campaigned with Richard of Gloucester in Scotland in the early 1480s, and some of their knightly supporters had seen action; but they would have relied heavily on the professionalism of Martin Schwartz and Richard Harliston. It was one thing to read Vegetius and practise swordsmanship on the training-ground, but quite another to know how, and when, to attack a determined enemy in unfamiliar country and to lead from the front into the teeth of a hail of arrows.

The Earl of Oxford's contingent would have consisted of a core of men-at-arms supported by archers and billmen in approximately equal numbers. They would all have been well-equipped, the professional men-at-arms (retainers) with full or part plate armour, and the archers and billmen with swords, bucklers (small round shields), helmets, brigandines or jacks (padded coats) and whatever pieces of plate or weaponry they had inherited from their fathers or scavenged from earlier battlefields. Martin Schwartz's troops would have been similarly well-accoutred (the 'marespikes' [Moorish pikes] 'gonnes' and [cross]'bowes' mentioned by the Act of Attainder were undoubtedly part of their weaponry), but the Irishmen were 'almost naked' (i.e. without body protection), and armed principally with 'skaynes' (skean dhu – literally 'black dagger' – as worn in the stocking by highlanders in full dress) and 'darts'.[18] Lincoln's English supporters were probably also less well-armed and harnessed than their counterparts in the royal army since, in many cases, they would have been unable to look to an overlord or to the town which had recruited them to make up deficiencies in their personal equipment. Some of them would have had longbows or bills (long staffs with hook-shaped blades), but others came armed with 'weapons' they used on a daily basis, hand-axes, mauls (heavy two-

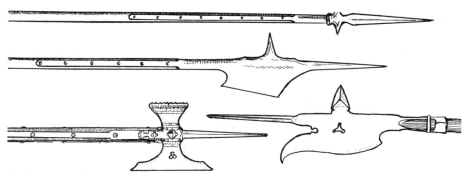

Staff weapons (from top) pike, halberd, bill and pole-axe.

handed hammers) and, of course, long knives. The rebel commanders would inevitably have experienced great difficulty in welding these disparate forces into a single coherent fighting unit, and would have found it still harder to make what had been planned on paper happen in practice. It would be fascinating to know something of their deployments, but all we are told by the chroniclers is that the experienced Swiss and Germans 'were in the front line'.[19]

Lincoln, Lovel and their colleagues had probably intended to hold the higher ground and fight a defensive battle as the royal commanders had supposed they would; but when they learned or realised that a substantial part of the royal army was still some distance from the battlefield they decided to throw their entire force against Oxford's smaller contingent while it was still deploying to either side of the Upper Fosse. They almost certainly knew of Jean de Bueil's warning that 'everywhere and on all occasions that foot-soldiers march against their enemy face to face, those who march lose and those who remain standing still holding firm win',[20] but probably felt that they had little alternative but to seize what might be their best chance of victory. At a little before nine o'clock the signal was given and they 'moved down to the fray' (Vergil), not in a headlong rush (which would have broken their formations) but resolutely, 'in good order'.[21] The mercenaries may have been deployed in mixed groups with the crossbowmen and handgunners protected by pikemen, or alternatively, may have been divided into separate units according to the weapons they carried. The crossbowmen and archers may have been positioned on the flanks of the German pikemen and English men-at-arms and billmen and advanced with them; but reloading while marching was inevitably slower than replenishing and discharging their weapons from a stationary position, and the bowmen may have been ordered to stop when within range of the enemy and give covering fire either between their comrades' contingents or over their heads.

Remaining in a fixed position would have obviated the need to adjust their range with each volley (which they would have had to do if they were moving forward), and would have compelled the royalists to aim either at them or at the approaching infantry rather than directing all their missiles at one body of men.

The ranges of the weapons used at Stoke would have depended upon their type and the skill and strength of those who used them, but at 400 yards, almost as soon as their advance had begun, the rebels would have come within range of any serpentines which Oxford had with him, and at between 250 and 300 yards would have encountered the potentially devastating arrow storm of the royal archers. These men would have stepped forward from their own ranks and fired as rapidly as possible, perhaps as many as ten arrows a minute, and although Lincoln's fewer missilemen answered according to whatever strategy the Earl had devised for them they could not match their enemies' fire-power. The crossbow was a powerful weapon which could penetrate plate armour at 80 yards if fired at right-angles to the target, but could deliver only two to four bolts per minute. The mercenaries' arquebuses could have been brought into use when they closed to within 200 yards of their enemies; but such was the time taken to clean and reload a handgun that each one was probably fired only once. Guns were, in any case, inaccurate at this distance, and the Germans (who were bound to discharge their weapons horizontally) may have been instructed to hold their fire until they were as little as 25–50 yards from the

Fifteenth-century woodcut of crossbowmen and handgunners.

Engraving of 'kerns' or professional Gaelic foot soldiers, attired in Irish mantles, brandishing broadswords and (right) a 'scian' or dagger.

royal army. The royal archers would have withdrawn behind the billmen by this time, and a salvo of armour-piercing bullets would have created gaps in the steel-tipped lines opposite – and caused even battle-hardened troops to recoil before them – in the crucial moments before the two forces clashed together.[22] The rebel gunners and bowmen themselves would then have retired to safety, although if the archers and crossbowmen had been ordered to halt some 250 yards from Oxford's battle (if, as we supposed, Lincoln had instructed them to fire rapidly from a standing position), they would have moved forward when they could no longer shoot without endangering their own soldiers. They would then have operated as snipers on the fringes of the conflict or laid aside their weapons and fought with side arms as light infantry in the mêlée.

The withering fire of Oxford's bowmen undoubtedly inflicted casualties on the rebels although some contingents were worse affected than others. The German crossbowmen could crouch behind their pavises (highly decorated tall shields, often carried by an assistant) and the English had various forms of protection; but the poorly harnessed Irish were more vulnerable and suffered considerable losses. It is likely that Lincoln and the other commanders had urged them to find something, however rudimentary, which would shelter them from incoming missiles (some of the Duke of Burgundy's archers had equipped themselves with doors taken from the village of Montlhéry at the commencement of the battle of that name twenty-two years earlier), but Molinet says that they were 'shot through and full of arrows like hedgehogs', and Hall adds that they were 'stryken downe and slayne lyke dull and brute beastes'.[23] The forces which Sir Thomas Geraldine had brought from Ireland are sometimes portrayed as an ill-equipped rabble whose need of sustenance and liking for plunder would have made it difficult for the rebel commanders to find adequate supplies and maintain discipline. But there is no evidence that they were hard to 'manage' or that their presence had slowed the army on its march through northern England; and although Vergil remarks that the losses they sustained 'struck no little terror into the other combatants'[24] he does not imply that they broke and fled. It would have been foolish to burden the army with men who were unlikely to give a good account of themselves, and the vast probability is that they were seasoned warriors who fought after the manner in which they and their ancestors had fought for centuries. Their weapons appeared primitive to their English adversaries, but few would have doubted their ability to use them effectively at close quarters in a sharp fight.

The two armies met with the clash of steel on steel with the shouts of the warriors and the cries of pain of the wounded adding to the noise of conflict. The royal men-at-arms and billmen, supported by the archers armed with swords and bucklers, did their best to avoid or deflect the thrusts of the Germans' long pikes and the deadly accurate 'darts' of the Irish, but were hard-pressed to hold their ground against these determined and unconventional opponents. Lord Bacon says that the struggle lasted for three hours, but it is unlikely that even the most seasoned campaigners could have wielded their heavy weapons continuously for such a long period. They almost certainly paused from time to time to recover, take a drink, and redress their lines (just as Oxford's and the Duke of Norfolk's forces had at Bosworth) before resuming the battle,[25] but with each pause the rebels' chances of breaking the royal position and releasing the 'inherent chaos' diminished. Oxford's troops may have been inferior in numbers but their greater overall professionalism now began to tell in their favour; and it was this superiority (together, perhaps, with the arrival of some men from the King's division) which eventually allowed them to move forward into the more ragged ranks of the Yorkists (perhaps 'in array tryangle'[26] or wedge formation, as at Bosworth) and push them back towards Stoke village. The retreat became a rout as the rebel position disintegrated, and quickly, perhaps within the space of a few minutes, it was quite literally 'every man for himself'.

Polydore Vergil says that Oxford's advance 'first of all caused the death of some of the enemy leaders offering resistance in various places' and implies that the ensuing alarm and despondency made it easier to 'put to flight the remainder'.[27] It is surprising that Lincoln, Schwartz, Sir Thomas Geraldine

A pavise (left) and crossbowman of the period.

and several of their principal knightly supporters all perished (Lincoln notwithstanding that Henry ·had wanted him spared for interrogation), and the only
logical explanation is that the suddenness and ferocity of Oxford's counter-
thrust gave them no opportunity either to surrender or to reach the horses they
had left tethered behind the army for just such an emergency. Francis Lovel
was the only senior rebel to escape the carnage, and it is possible to surmise that
he had been given command of a small mounted reserve (consisting, probably,
of most of the few horsemen the Yorkists had with them) which doubled as a
bodyguard for 'King Edward' and which remained stationed on the higher
ground when the main army moved forward. This was not brought into the
action, presumably because the opportunity for which it had been saved failed
to present itself, and its members were able to ride to safety when it became
apparent that the battle was lost.

This reconstruction has tried to take account of a number of alternative deployments and strategies, but there were others which could also have been utilised. One possibility is that, given time, the Earl of Oxford could have extended his line eastwards into Elston fields to prevent the rebels from out-flanking him. The problem was that this would have spread his men more thinly while making it difficult for the King's forces to deploy when they arrived on the battlefield; and he may have concluded that it was preferable to order the archers on his right to hold their positions and shoot at an angle while those stationed on the left and in the centre aimed directly ahead.[28] He may have hoped that the superior fire-power of his forces would, in any case, reduce the odds against him before the battle came to hand-strokes, and there was a chance that a serious hand-to-hand conflict might be avoided altogether. It is possible that nearly half the Earl's 6,000 men were archers – a rough estimate of his strength would be 400 men-at-arms, 2,800 bowmen and the same number of billmen[29] – and that each bowman could, as we noted earlier, have fired as many as ten arrows per minute. Some three minutes would have elapsed between the advancing rebels coming within bowshot at 250–300 yards and the royal archers retiring behind their own billmen when their enemies approached to within perhaps 25–50 yards, long enough for the royalists to shoot as many as 84,000 arrows (2,800 men launching ten arrows per man per minute) into their opponents' ranks.[30] This figure would not have been possible if each archer carried only a single sheaf of twenty-four arrows as was customary, but if each man fired only, say, twenty missiles (keeping a few back for a later emergency), it was still enough to annihilate the entire Yorkist army many times over. It was only on rare occasions that archers could win a battle almost single-handedly, but such devastating fire-power *could* have brought the rebel attack to a standstill and forced some units, particularly the poorly harnessed Irish, to retire. Lincoln and some of the other slain commanders could have perished in the arrow storm (this would explain why it was not possible to heed the King's order to take him alive for questioning), and the royal men-at-arms and billmen would have had little difficulty in overwhelming forces which were already partially broken and leaderless. The main objection to this scenario is Bacon's statement that the battle lasted for three hours, far longer than would have been needed to overcome an army which had already been demoralised by heavy casualties; but it is typical of the permutations which have to be considered if we are to form any real picture of what happened that day.

The majority of the rebel soldiers would have scattered when their lines broke – forces which lacked natural cohesion always disintegrated more easily in these circumstances – and Oxford would have lost no time in ordering his mounted troops to pursue them and complete the victory. No writer describes

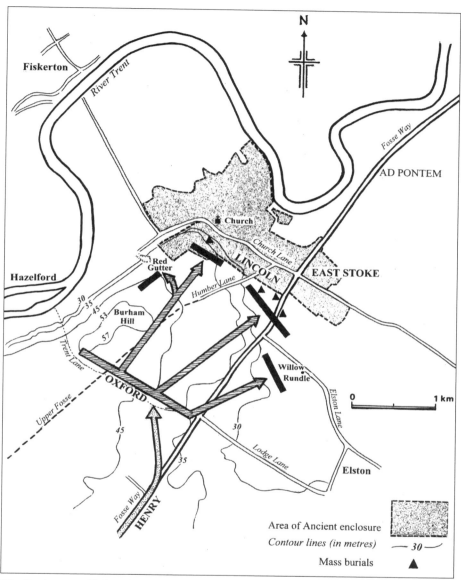

The Battle, noon, 16 June 1487.

this stage of the conflict, but archaeological evidence suggests that some of the fugitives made for the gully in the escarpment leading to Fiskerton while others ran towards the Fosse Way or tried to escape through the enclosures around the village. Mass burials have been discovered in all these locations (see Map 3), and there can be little doubt that at least some of them are the graves of men who were caught by the victorious royalists and cut down as they fled. St Oswald's church offered the prospect of sanctuary to those fortunate enough to reach it, but the privilege may not have been respected in these circumstances. Edward IV had executed some of his Lancastrian enemies after dragging them from Tewkesbury Abbey sixteen years earlier, and the same fate may have awaited any senior Yorkists who were found clinging to the altar after Stoke. The 'servaunt of Master Recordour' who galloped into York at 3 am the following morning reported that 5,000 rebels had been 'slayne *and murdred*'[31] (my italics), and although his sum can only have been a rough estimate it is broadly consistent with the more considered total of 4,000 deaths recorded by the herald. Molinet goes so far as to assert that only 200 rebels escaped and that even some of these were captured and executed in the days which followed. His figure is probably again based on a misunderstanding, but there is no reason to doubt his comment that although English and Irish prisoners (Henry's subjects) were executed, the surviving foreign mercenaries were allowed to return to the Continent. The Irish fugitives probably fared worse since they were now many miles from the sea and had nowhere to hide in England. A few may have straggled back to Ireland eventually, but most of those who had sailed with Lincoln and Geraldine probably never saw their homeland again.

There is no corresponding estimate of how many royalist soldiers fell in the battle. Some writers argue for a very small number of casualties, but more may be inferred from Edward Hall's comment that 'not halfe of them whych fougthe in the forward and gave the onset (were) slayne or hurt'.[32] This would suggest a figure approaching 3,000, included wounded, and perhaps several hundred fatalities, but if so, it is surprising that no one of consequence seems to have been killed or suffered serious injury. In any event there were now plenty of men from the King's division available to join in the pursuit of the fleeing rebels, and their victory was completed by the capture of Simnel and the priest Simons. These two, whom their own men had presumably not thought worth saving or rescuing, were taken 'by a vaylent (valiant) and gentil esquier of the King's howse called Robert Bellingham'[33] and consigned to oblivion – the boy, with wry humour, to the royal kitchens and his mentor to prison. Oxford and the King (who had probably followed, rather than led, his own men into action) made their way to Burham Hill and marked their victory by raising the royal standard over the ground where the rebels had stood a few hours earlier. But

Henry then left almost immediately – 'without dismounting' according to Molinet[34] – leaving others to oversee the care of the wounded and the burial of the fallen. Villagers may have helped the soldiers dig grave pits (all of them with an eye to whatever articles of value could be removed from the corpses in the process), and soon, perhaps within a matter of hours, much of the 'evidence' for the battle had disappeared for ever. The Yorkist party had been decimated, and although pretenders, real and imaginary, continued to trouble Henry for more than a decade, the threat was never as serious again.

Chapter 6

When the Dust Settled

Molinet says that immediately after the battle Henry went to Newark, where the clergy of the 'great church' (St Mary Magdalene) came to meet him and where he 'hailed the Virgin Mary and gave his standard to the image of St George'.[1] He probably passed the rest of the day in the town before marching to Lincoln, some 20 miles distant, on Sunday 'taking with him a number of captives whom he punished by death'.[2] Vergil does not explain who these men were or why they were spared for a day or two rather than killed on the battlefield. Perhaps they were Englishmen who had been close to John de la Pole or Francis Lovel and from whom the King hoped to gather some of the information he had meant to extract from the ringleaders if they had been taken alive as intended. He then sent Christopher Urswick with another of his standards (or perhaps his personal banner) to the shrine of Our Lady at Walsingham in Norfolk before disbanding all but 4,000–5,000 of his soldiers on Monday. By the end of the month he was back at Kenilworth, and remained there until the beginning of August, when he set out for York and the north.

It was probably at Newark that Henry rewarded some of those who had distinguished themselves in the battle by creating nine new bannerets and by dubbing many of the knights bachelor named by the herald. He also sent letters to York and other places instructing them to hold services of thanksgiving for his victory, although whether this was the message carried by the 'servaunt of Master Recordour' or a second, official notification, is uncertain. York is 76 miles from Newark and would normally have been reckoned as two days' journey. A messenger who left at midday on Saturday, as soon as the battle was decided, would have been hard-pressed to reach his destination by 3 am the following morning, and it would have been still more difficult for one who did not leave Newark until late afternoon.

Henry also notified foreign rulers of his triumph during the weeks which followed, and his letter to one of these, Pope Innocent VIII, makes interesting reading. The King wanted to tighten the rules governing sanctuary and make life difficult for the Irish bishops and archbishops who had supported Simnel; and Pope Innocent, whose office had been diminished by the 'Babylonish Captivity' of Avignon, the Great Schism, and the failure of the Conciliar

Movement, was ready to assist a ruler
who was prepared to treat the papacy
with the respect it had enjoyed in
earlier centuries. One of those who had
emerged from the Westminster sanctuary to plunder the property of known
royal sympathisers when Lord Welles's
retreat gave rise to rumours that Henry
had been defeated was an otherwise
obscure individual named John Swit.
Swit had allegedly boasted that papal
support for Henry counted for nothing.
'And what signify censures of church or
pontiff?' he harangued his comrades,
'Do you not perceive that interdicts of
this sort are of no weight whatever,
since you see with your own eyes that
those very men who obtained such in
their own favour are routed, and that
the whole anathema has recoiled upon
their own heads?' It gave Henry no
little pleasure to inform Pope Innocent
that 'on pronouncing these words he
instantly fell down dead upon the
ground, and his face and body immediately became blacker than soot
itself, and shortly afterwards emitted
such a stench that no one soever could
approach it.'[3] God was clearly on the
King's (and the Pope's) side!

Henry's success seems to have convinced him that he could now crown
his wife Elizabeth, Edward IV's daughter, as his queen. Elizabeth's title to
the throne was arguably better than
her husband's, and although she was
already the mother of Prince Arthur he
was acutely conscious that he had been
obliged to swear an oath to marry her
in order to persuade some of Richard

*Memorial brass to Sir Richard Fitzlewis,
knighted at Stoke (Ingrave, Essex).*

III's enemies to give him their allegiance. He was prepared to do what was necessary to persuade former Yorkists to support him, but any suggestion that he ruled England in right of, or on behalf of, his wife was an entirely different matter. The coronation only took place (in November 1487) when he considered that he had made this point to his own satisfaction, and although kings did not normally attend the service when a queen was crowned separately, Henry and his ever-present mother watched the proceedings from behind a screen!

The crowning of the young Queen probably satisfied one of the grievances of the Queen Mother, Elizabeth Woodville, but Henry's victory had effectively nullified her ambitions. He preserved the fiction that he would marry her to James III, King of Scots (doubtless to help keep the peace on his northern border), until James was killed in June 1488, but she remained immured in Bermondsey Abbey until her death in 1492. She was not permitted to attend her daughter's coronation, and her only contact with the court was an occasion in November 1489 when she was allowed to meet her kinsman Francois de Luxembourg, who was visiting London at the head of a French embassy. The gathering was strictly formal, carefully supervised by Henry's mother, and Elizabeth was given no opportunity to plead or protest her lot in a quiet corner. Some writers take the view that, because Henry referred to her in endearing language in the grants he provided for her maintenance, he was actually on good terms with her. But such expressions were politely conventional, and his treatment of her, and the penury of her last will and testament, say more about their relationship than any words.[4]

The need to keep up appearances meant that Henry could not subject his mother-in-law to due legal process, nor could he impose the full weight of the law on the senior clergymen who had supported the rebellion. Little more is heard of Robert Stillington, Bishop of Bath and Wells, who may have been kept under surveillance until he died, four years after the battle; and although John Sante, Abbot of Abingdon, avoided detection on this occasion he was attainted for his part in a hare-brained scheme to free the real Earl of Warwick in 1489. He was pardoned in February 1493, however, and forgiveness was also extended to Nicholas Boston, Prior of Tynemouth (who had been bound under 500 marks in April 1487), to four heads of northern religious houses, and to Archdeacon Ralph Booth of York, although they all paid fines above 100 marks when the King visited the region after the rebellion. We do not know how most of these last had actually offended Henry, but Archdeacon Booth, Abbot William Sever of St Mary's, York, and Abbot John Darneton of Fountains may have joined with Abbot William Heslyngton of Jervaulx in offering Lincoln some practical assistance, while Prior John Aukland of Durham (whose house was more distant) had presumably made encouraging noises.[5] They all kept their positions, of course, as did Richard Redman, Bishop of St Asaph, who, besides being translated to Exeter and then Ely (as we noticed earlier) was even appointed to the Privy Council in 1493.

John, Lord Scrope of Bolton, was the most senior English peer involved in the uprising after Lincoln and Lovel, but his part in it had been equivocal and he was treated with appropriate leniency. He came south in the immediate aftermath of the rebellion (either voluntarily or in response to a royal summons), and on 26 August was imprisoned in Windsor Castle and bound under £3,000 for his future behaviour. Four knights stood surety for him and agreed to forfeit £2,000 each if he defaulted, but he was formally pardoned only six months later on 5 February 1488. He was released shortly afterwards on condition that he did not travel more than 22 miles from Windsor, and was licensed to reside anywhere in southern England on 2 July 1489. Interestingly, he was again bound under 12,000 marks when Duchess Margaret's next protégé, Perkin Warbeck, began to threaten Henry in November 1491, but fought against the Scots and assisted in raising the siege of Norham Castle the year before he died, on 17 August 1498.[6] The King may never have entirely trusted him, but perhaps finally accepted that he was unlikely to cause trouble again.

Similar strictures were also applied to John's kinsman, Lord Thomas Scrope, and to their supporter Sir Edmund Hastings. Thomas was similarly bound in August 1487 and imprisoned at Wallingford, but he was licensed to go up to 22 miles from the castle in April 1488 and his sureties were discharged. He was again bound under 5,000 marks (presumably to deter him from helping Warbeck) in February 1492, but was retained to serve overseas with one man-at-arms, fifteen horse, and fifteen foot-archers shortly before he died, aged only about thirty-four, on 23 April 1493.[7] Edmund Hastings was bound under £2,000 and detained in Colchester Castle in August 1487, but he was pardoned in December and appointed a tax assessor for the North Riding of Yorkshire in the new year. His career looked set to recover, but like Thomas Scrope he died early, at some time before April 1489.[8]

The penalties meted out to the lesser rebels fortunate enough to survive the battle also seem to have been relatively lenient, and some even prospered under the government they had tried to diminish. It would be a lengthy – and perhaps rather dull – exercise to seek to examine what became of everyone we suspect was involved in the uprising, but the twenty-eight individuals who were attainted by the November parliament stand apart from the broad mass of rebel sympathisers and afford some insight into how Henry dealt with his opponents. The Earl of Lincoln had been killed, of course, and so too, probably, had most of the fourteen others whose names effectively disappear from the record: Sir

val Kings. Henry VII (Society of Antiquaries) and remains of seal of 'Edward VI' with
sh groats struck in his name (from *Hermathena*, no. 144 (1988)).

he Commanders. Seals of John de la Pole, Earl of Lincoln and John de Vere, Earl of Oxford.

Scheming Ladies. Margaret, Duchess of Burgundy (Society of Antiquaries), and Queen Elizabeth Woodville, a portrait in the Deanery, Ripon.

Northern Enemies. Garter Stall Plates of Henry Percy, Earl of Northumberland, and Francis Viscount Lovel (both St George's Chapel, Windsor).

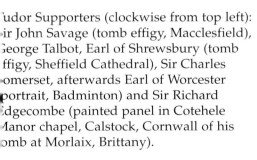

Tudor Supporters (clockwise from top left): Sir John Savage (tomb effigy, Macclesfield), George Talbot, Earl of Shrewsbury (tomb effigy, Sheffield Cathedral), Sir Charles Somerset, afterwards Earl of Worcester (portrait, Badminton) and Sir Richard Edgecombe (painted panel in Cotehele Manor chapel, Calstock, Cornwall of his tomb at Morlaix, Brittany).

Contending Clergy. Tomb of Richard Redman, Bishop of St Asaph, in Ely Catherdral (Rebekah Beale), and brass commemorating Christopher Urswick, Archdeacon of Richmond and Dean of Windsor, at Hackney, Middlesex.

Garter Stall Plate of John, Lord Scrope of Bolton (St George's Chapel, Windsor), and Bolton Castle, Wensleydale, the scene of anxious discussion in 1487. (Joyce Baldwin)

Royal standard of Henry VII.

Burham Hill and ridge, the position occupied by the rebels immediately prior to the battle, viewed from where the Earl of Oxford's right wing was stationed near Trent Lane. (Joyce Baldwin)

The 'Burrand Bush' memorial stone.

umber Lane as it approaches Stoke llage, all that remains of the 'Upper osse'. (Joyce Baldwin)

The 'Red Gutter'. (Joyce Baldwin)

Modern memorial stone, St Oswald's church, south wall of tower.

St Oswald's church, East Stoke.

Willow Rundle, the 'well' of Stoke battlefield. (Joyce Baldwin)

Fiskerton, viewed from the Stoke bank of the river Trent. (Joyce Baldwin)

Human remains found south of the village in 1982 (Nottinghamshire County Council Historic Environment Record) and engraving of spur found on the battlefield *c.* 1825.

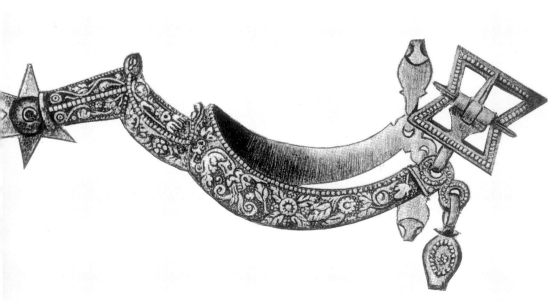

Minster Lovel Hall and (insets)
Lovel fording the Trent and the
skeleton in the vault (artist's
impressions).

Henry Bodrugan and Sir Thomas Broughton, together with John Beaumont, Thomas Harrington, Thomas Batell, Richard Middleton, Edmund Juse, William Kay, three of the four Mallarys, Robert Manning, Richard Hoigesson (Hodgson) and John Avantry. At least two others, Edward Frank and Thomas Blandrehasset, were imprisoned, although Frank was released from the Tower at some time before the following February and Blandrehasset was formally pardoned on 1 July 1488.[9] The latter was unfortunate inasmuch as he probably knew more about the conspiracy than most of the survivors (he was one of those who had slipped abroad with Lincoln in March 1487), and forgiven or not, he remained in custody 'at the King's pleasure'.[10] Robert Percy, John Broughton, Robert Hilton, John Mallary and Roger Hartlington were also granted pardons at dates between February 1488 and October 1489, while Rowland Robinson obtained his with the help of the Durham peer Lord Lumley, some time in the sixth year of the pontificate of Pope Innocent VIII (29 August 1489 to 28 August 1490). Percy, Hilton and Mallary (and probably all six of them) recovered their goods and chattels, but there is no indication that they were restored to their properties. Hilton's holdings in Halliwell and Smithell (Lancashire) were included in a package of forfeited estates granted to Henry's step-father, the Earl of Derby, in February 1489, while Henry Huddleston, who had resisted the King after Bosworth but who was now a 'gentleman of the chamber', was given a life interest in Broughton's lands in Cumberland. Sir John Turberville, described as the King's 'knight marshal', was granted Mallary's manor of Litchborough in Northamptonshire only two months after the battle, and Henry probably kept whatever he had seized from Percy, Hartlington and Robinson. The wording of the grant to Turberville 'and to the heires of his body lawfully comyng for ever' suggests that however hard Mallary worked to prove his loyalty to the new dynasty there was little likelihood that he would recover Litchborough, and the King's gift of the reversion of Huddleston's life interest in Broughton's lands to his own step-father meant that Broughton had no prospect of restoration either.[11] Their forgiveness was limited, and they would have had to live with the fact that they had backed the wrong side.

There were, however, four who were attainted in 1487 who were able to put the past behind them and forge new and worthwhile careers. Alexander Appleby was already a gentleman usher of the King's chamber when his royal master granted him two farms in the lordship of Penrith on 3 August 1490; and Clement Skelton was described as a 'king's servant' when given, rent free, 'certain lands and tenements called Blenkkogo, in the parish of Brownfeld, Co. Cumberland' in June 1494.[12] They had clearly commended themselves to King Henry, and it would be fascinating to know why they were not only pardoned but rewarded and given places in his household. James Harrington the younger, Sir Robert's son, entered the Church and the Earl of Derby allowed his presentation to the rectory of his father's forfeited manor of Badsworth. He was appointed sub-dean of York in 1508 and advanced to the deanery by Archbishop Bainbridge the year following, but his health deteriorated so rapidly that the Chapter excused him from attending the Minster in 1510. They provided him with a marble stone bearing a brass inscription when he died two years later, but it is now, unfortunately, lost.[13] Very little is known of Richard Banke, but he was apparently also at liberty and prospering when he leased the watermill of Bellwith Rosset and appurtenances, in the lordship of Knaresborough, Yorkshire, in February 1488.[14]

The only rebels who, so far as is known, continued to resist Henry were Edward Frank and Rowland Robinson (although the former had been set free and the latter pardoned) together with Richard Harliston, the former governor of Jersey. Frank was party to the abortive scheme to liberate Edward, Earl of Warwick which resulted in Abbot Sante's attainder in 1489, while Robinson and Harliston both entered the service of Margaret of Burgundy and supported Perkin Warbeck. A sixteenth-century Jersey chronicler wrote that Margaret convinced Harliston that Warbeck was Richard, Duke of York, the younger of the 'princes in the Tower', and he was among those attainted after an attempted landing at Deal (Kent) failed disastrously in July 1495. Robinson regularly carried letters between Margaret and King James IV of Scotland, and was appropriately rewarded by James for his trouble. He rode to the Anglo-Scottish border to rally support for Warbeck shortly before he and James invaded England in September 1496, and was given £200 by the King to pay off some of his young master's supporters after their ignominious withdrawal. He brought James word that Perkin had landed in Cornwall a year later, but interestingly, did not then rejoin him – he seems to have been one of life's survivors and may have guessed that the game was all but over.[15] He is last heard of receiving a final payment of 30s 9d from the King in December and may have then made his way back to the court of Burgundy. Richard Harliston certainly lived out his life in Flanders as Margaret's pensioner, and when he died there was buried honourably at her expense.[16]

It was inevitable that some rebels would pay a high price for their disloyalty, but finishing on the winning side did not guarantee unlimited favour either. Robert Bellingham, the 'valiant and gentle esquire' who had captured Simnel, sought the hand of Margery Ruyton, the widow of a wealthy Coventry merchant, but his suit was (presumably) rejected by her father, John Beaufitz of Temple Balsall (Warks.) Margery had lived at Temple Balsall since her husband's death, and at about suppertime on 2 September 1487 Bellingham entered the property with more than twenty accomplices, threatened the servants, and rode off carrying Margery with him. Margery seems to have been willing to marry Bellingham and may even have enjoyed the excitement; but the King was angered by the young suitor's disrespect for rights and property and incarcerated him in Warwick prison. The case against him collapsed when he was tried the following July (probably he had used the interval to make his peace with the affronted Beaufitz), and he began to rebuild his career in Henry's service. He was appointed bailiff of the royal estate at Sutton in Warwickshire in 1494 and was serving as sergeant-porter two years later. The King doubtless felt some obligation towards him, but this did not extend to overlooking breaches of the law.[17]

The Bellingham case illustrates King Henry's determination to stamp his authority on his newly won kingdom, but it also typifies the confusion which can arise when two men with identical names appear in the record. One of Sir Robert's accomplices in the attack on Temple Balsall was a Rowland Robinson whose domicile is given as of Berkswell (Warks.), only six miles from Bellingham's home at Kenilworth. It is sometimes assumed that he was the Rowland Robinson who joined the Simnel rebellion and subsequently helped Perkin Warbeck, but the evidence suggests that the rebel Robinson was a Durham man, described in his pardon as 'late of the Isle, near Bradbery, yeoman'.[18] It seems unlikely that the individual arrested with Bellingham and found not guilty when their case came to trial in July 1488 had been attainted of high treason in the interval, and still more improbable that the man who helped Sir Robert abduct Margery Ruyton had fought against him at Stoke less than two months earlier. In the final analysis there is no absolute proof that we are dealing with two Rowland Robinsons, but it would be remarkable if just one of them could conform to so many apparently conflicting facts.[19]

Bellingham was, no doubt, duly chastened, but a worse fate awaited Henry Percy, Earl of Northumberland. Northumberland had neatly side-stepped the troubles of 1487, but when, two years later, the King ordered him to deal with a protest mounted against a demand for a new tax on moveable property, he had little alternative but to comply. He met the protestors, from Ayton in Cleveland, at Cocklodge, near Thirsk, on 28 April, and such was the mob's fury that he was dragged from his horse and murdered without his retainers – who were presumably as disillusioned – raising a hand to save him. They had all doubtless expected him to intercede with the King, to exercise his 'good lordship' to ameliorate the burden upon them, and felt betrayed when he merely tried to enforce it; but it is also possible that some of them still resented his failure to support Richard III at Bosworth. Dr Cunningham suggests that Henry may have wanted to place former Ricardians who had joined Northumberland's retinue in a situation which would test their loyalty to the new government, or alternatively, may have wished to demonstrate that Northumberland 'was first and foremost a servant of the Crown, that his power was derived directly from the King, and that his position in the north depended on his continued good service.'[20] He would not have expected his schemes to have ended so dramatically and bloodily, however, and it is a measure of his concern that he entered Yorkshire in May with a larger army than he had recruited before Stoke. The rebels gained access to York on the 15th but withdrew two days later as the King approached. There were six executions, and bonds and sureties were required of those who might have done more to oppose the insurgents than they had.

Henry was prepared to deal firmly with recalcitrant Englishmen, but was obliged to take an altogether more conciliatory approach towards his Irish rebels. His letter to Pope Innocent, written on 5 July 1487, complained of the conduct of 'certain Irish bishops, namely the Archbishops of Dublin and Armagh and the Bishops of Meath and Kildare' who had joined the rebellion against him, and asked the Holy Father 'to cite them, as having incurred the censures of the Church.' The Pope was, as we saw, happy to oblige him, and wrote to the Archbishops of Tuam and Cashel, and to the Bishops of Clogher and Ossory, on 5 January ordering them to collect information against the accused prelates and to forward it to him. He later issued a bull, *Contra Rebelles Domini Regis*, which forbade any rebellion against Henry under pain of excommunication, and declared that the people of Ireland were expressly included in the order. But that seems to have been largely the end of the matter since Henry pardoned the four prelates together with the Bishop of Cloyne, twenty-eight other clergy, lords and officers, and 'the whole commonalty of the city of Dublin and the town or borough of Drogheda' on 25 May 1488. The townsmen of Kinsale had been similarly forgiven nine days before.[21]

Henry had written to Maurice Fitzgerald, Earl of Desmond, (who had apparently not supported the uprising) in April ordering him to arrest any rebels he could find in Ireland, but there is no evidence that he was able to do so. The arch-rebel was, of course, Gerald, the Earl of Kildare, Desmond's kinsman, who had been included in the 25 May pardon, presumably because Henry recognised that military action would be needed to censure or remove him and because his considerable influence in the country might still benefit the House of Tudor. The King decided to invoke his own feudal and moral authority, however, and Sir Richard Edgecombe (Bodrugan's protagonist) was despatched to Ireland in the summer with instructions to exact a new oath of allegiance from everyone of note. On 27 June Edgecombe landed at Kinsale, where he administered the oath to Lord de Courcy and Viscount Barry, and then travelled to Waterford, where he was received and entertained warmly. Henry had written to Waterford in October 1487 thanking the citizens for their devotion to him during the uprising and authorising them to seize and detain rebel ships.

So far, so good, but Dublin, whither Sir Richard sailed on 5 July, was less friendly territory. A number of Irish lords waited upon him, but Kildare, he was informed, had gone on a pilgrimage and would be away for some days. When the Earl returned on the 12th he desired Edgecombe to come to him, rather than vice-versa, and although Sir Richard concurred to avoid friction he displayed his (and presumably Henry's) displeasure by offering him none of the usual courtesies when they met. He concentrated instead on reading the oath of allegiance which the King required the assembled notables to swear to him, and may or may not have been surprised when they declared one clause in particular to be wholly unacceptable and asked for a five-day postponement.[22] He was obliged to modify the point in question to secure their agreement when they next met on the 21st, and took the precaution of requiring them to hold their hands over a host consecrated by his own chaplain to avoid any possibility of trickery and subsequent evasion. Kildare then swore allegiance followed by, among others, great Darcy of Platten, who had carried Simnel on his shoulders, and John Payne, Bishop of Meath, who had outlined the boy's claim to the throne at his coronation and had been 'punished' by being required to read aloud the Pope's excommunication and the terms of the King's pardon. Spiritual censures may have carried more weight than the unlikely threat of an English invasion, and although Sir Richard placed a gold chain around Kildare's neck (formally confirming him in his office of Lord Deputy) at the end of the ceremony, he cannot have supposed that the relationship between his royal master and the majority of the Anglo-Irish peerage had significantly altered. Trust was also at a premium when, next day, he administered the oath to the mayor and leading citizens. They all swore loyalty to King Henry, but were collectively fined 1,000 marks with the proviso that they would not have to pay it 'if they maintained their allegiance and fealty unbroken and unshaken'. Edgecombe probably felt he had done his best and could look forward to a pleasant journey home when he left Dublin on 30 July, but his eight-day voyage to Fowey in Cornwall proved as stormy as anything he had encountered while he had been away.

Kildare and his associates came to London the following year (1489) in response to a royal summons, and were accused of gullibility rather than disloyalty. 'My masters of Ireland, you will crown apes at length', Henry chided them, and later, when they were at dinner, a gentleman came 'and told them that their new King Lambarte Symenell brought them wine to drink, and

Engraving of the tomb of Gerald, eighth Earl of Kildare in St Mary's Chapel, Christchurch Cathedral, Dublin, destroyed in the seventeenth century, and detail of tomb slab, showing the family crests and arms, supported by two apes, which may have given rise to King Henry's remark about 'crowning apes'.

drank to them all'. 'None would have taken the cup out of his hands, but bade the great Devil of Hell him take before that ever they saw him', says the chronicler; but the Lord of Howth (who had never recognised the pretender and who clearly enjoyed his colleagues' embarrassment) told Simnel to serve him 'if the wine be good . . . and I shall drink it off for the wine's sake and mine own sake also; and for thee, as thou art, so I leave thee, a poor innocent.'[23] Kildare seems to have portrayed himself as a likeable rogue who should be forgiven any misdemeanour. When, on another occasion, he came to England to settle a dispute with the Bishop of Meath, he behaved with such familiarity towards Henry, taking his hand and telling him amusing stories, that the court was altogether won over. 'All Ireland cannot rule yonder gentleman', said the Bishop despairingly. 'No?' replied the King, 'Them he is meet to rule all Ireland, seeing all Ireland cannot rule him.'[24] There is no independent confirmation that these events actually happened or happened in the way in which *The Book of Howth* describes them, but they are surely worth repeating for their own sake.

And what of Simnel, the boy of uncertain identity who, for a few weeks, doubtless believed he was to become King of England? Henry, as we have seen, treated him kindly, if contemptuously, by setting him to work in the royal kitchens; but the *presence* which had made him a plausible Plantagenet also helped him to rise to the position of King's Falconer. He is almost certainly the 'Lambert Symnell yeoman' who attended Sir Thomas Lovel's funeral in May 1525, and Vergil indicates that he was still living when the first printed edition

Victorian engraving of Lambert Simnel as a 'scullion' in the royal kitchens.

of the *Anglica Historia* was published in 1534. He may even have married and had children since a Richard Simnell, canon of St Osyth's in Essex, was awarded a pension of £100 when his house was dissolved on 8 August 1539.[25] It has been suggested that the conspiracy originated in Richard III's reign in response to the disappearance of Edward V and Richard, Duke of York, (this would, perhaps, explain why Lambert's identity was subsequently changed from York to Warwick), and also that he may have been one of the missing 'princes' or the real Earl of Warwick. One theory is that the boy crowned in Dublin was actually Edward V, and it was only when he was killed at Stoke Field that King Henry substituted Simnel (probably with the connivance of Robert Bellingham) in order to prove to everyone that he was plainly an impostor.[26] It is not clear how Henry hoped to benefit from this, however, and even if he had managed to contrive it he would surely have realised that he could not fool everyone. The vast probability is that Lambert was an ordinary boy who became a pawn in the hands of powerful Yorkists, and it is likely that, from the comfort and security of his later years as a senior royal servant, he looked back with some pleasure on his few weeks as an English king.

Chapter 7

The Disappearance of Lord Lovel

Francis Lovel turned his horse and rode away from the battlefield when it became apparent that the day was lost for the Yorkists, but no one knew where he had gone or what had become of him. Perhaps, at first, it was assumed that he had fled into hiding, but as time passed it became apparent that his disappearance was permanent and that some mischance had befallen him. Commentators were baffled and speculated that he might have drowned crossing the Trent or somehow starved to death immured in his own cellar, but their suggestions, and reported sightings of him in Scotland and elsewhere in Europe, only added to the mystery. Lovel is not an Edward II or a Richard II, still less a King Arthur; but his friendship with Richard III and the few details of his life which are known with certainty have combined to make him a romantic and intriguing figure, someone whose end, if it did not affect the course of history, is still worth considering for its own sake.[1]

There are many references to Lovel's fate in documents composed, in the main, within a generation of the rebellion; and the problem is not so much a lack of 'evidence' but rather how much reliance can be placed upon it. One story we can dispose of fairly easily is the report of *The Great Chronicle of London* – a work often considered one of the more valuable sources for the period – that Lovel met his death at Bosworth in 1485. There is no doubt that he survived this battle, and indeed, lived to fight at Stoke two years later; and the most likely explanation is that the writer was misled by the new government's own propaganda. The York city archives preserve a letter[2] received from Henry VII a few days after Bosworth in which Lovel and other prominent Yorkists who survived the conflict are reported killed, probably, as Professor Kendall surmises, to discourage resistance in other parts of the country.[3] That the chronicler, far removed from the scene of events, believed such stories is understandable; but the failure of later copyists to correct the error (the chronicle does not appear to have been put into its present form until some time between 1496 and 1510), shows how cautiously such histories must be used.

But perhaps the easiest way for early-sixteenth-century writers to explain Lovel's disappearance was simply to assume that he had been killed at the battle of Stoke. The first to do so was the London merchant Richard Arnold, whose brief *Chronicle* was first published in 1502: and by the time Polydore Vergil completed the first draft of his *Anglica Historia* a decade or so later it had become the officially accepted view.[4] Lovel, they supposed, had simply been overlooked when the dead were buried, although he could have been identified by any one of several relatives and associates who had fought for King Henry – his brother-in-law Sir Edward Norris (husband of his sister Frideswide), his former colleague Sir William Stonor, and his cousin Henry Lovel, Lord Morley, his father's brother's son.[5] But the slain were soon despoiled of anything of value, and it was quite possible that Lovel, stripped of the trappings of nobility and disfigured, perhaps, by wounds received in the battle, had been interred unnoticed in one of the mass graves on the battlefield. Mathieu d'Escouchy tells of how, on the day after Castillon, the body of the renowned John Talbot was 'much changed' in appearance, and was only identified with certainty when a follower recognised an imperfection in his late master's teeth.[6] Clearly, when Lovel had been missing for more than a quarter of a century, those who had no interest in pursuing the matter were entitled to presume that anonymity had indeed been his fate.

But there are other notices, written, in some cases, within months rather than years of the battle, which show that Vergil's apparent certainty masked a far more complicated story. The one writer with at least some first-hand knowledge of the encounter, the unnamed herald who accompanied the Tudor army, reported, 'The Vicount Lorde Lovell [was] put to flight', and the closely contemporary College of Arms MS 2M6 (printed under the title 'Historical notes of a London citizen') adds, 'with money (many) other ientilmen too'.[7] Both documents name some of the leading rebels who were slain or captured in the fighting, and the inference is clearly that Lovel made good his escape. The oft-repeated story that he drowned while swimming his horse across the Trent at Fiskerton, although a good way of explaining the absence of a body, is probably of somewhat later provenance. It does not appear in literature until Edward Hall included it in his *Chronicle* in 1542.

There is, moreover, evidence which implies that Lovel not only survived the conflict, but was thought to be still living as late as the beginning of the next decade. British Library Vitellius A XVI, a chronicle compiled, probably, about 1490, has appended a very full list of the 'Names of dyvers lordis, knyghtes, and gentilmen, the which have ben slayn in the Realme of England Sith (since) the good Duke of Glowcestre was mourdred at the parlement holden at Bury'[8] (i.e. February 1447), from which Lovel is specifically omitted. The scribe recorded that, together with the Earl of Lincoln and Martin Schwartz, he 'cam to Stoke feeld', but only Schwartz and Lincoln are subsequently listed as slain.

Equally significant is the wording of the grants by which the Crown disposed of certain of Henry Lovel's holdings following his death at Dixmude in 1489, lands which 'would have descended to Fraunceys late viscounte Lovell, had not the last-named lord forfeited his right and title to the same by reason of his attainder of high treason against the king'.[9] The term 'late viscount' means simply that he was no longer a member of the peerage (Thomas Howard, for example, is sometimes described as 'late Earl of Surrey' prior to his rehabilitation in 1489);[10] and there would have been no need for the King to use the proscription as a legal excuse to take possession of the properties (unless, of course, he wished to frustrate the claims of Lovel's two sisters) if Francis had indisputably predeceased his cousin. It is impossible to know whether these authorities had real grounds for presuming that Lovel was still living; but they were clearly prepared to countenance the possibility for several years after he had supposedly died.

There were, however, others who claimed they *knew* that Lovel had survived the battle or who tried to assist him for some time afterwards. Sheilah O'Connor has drawn attention to a letter of safe conduct which James IV, King of Scots, issued to Lovel and other named fugitives on 19 June 1488, authorising them, their servants, and others who were of the same opinion to enter Scotland for one year certain and then at his pleasure.[11] There is no proof that any of them accepted the offer, but it is curious that in July 1491 the Mayor of York wrote to advise Sir Richard Tunstall that he had

> 'takyn a sympill and pure person and commyt him to prison the which went about here in your Citie, and shewid and utterd to diverse persons within ye same that he spak with ye lord Lovell . . . in Scotland, howbeit afor me he denyeth that he never so said ne shewid, and what your maistershup thinks I shuld doo forther herein, I pray you send me word.'[12]

The 'sympill' person was at least wise enough to deny the story when the Mayor interviewed him; but whether he had really seen Lovel within the preceding three years (or was just repeating an old rumour) is unfortunately impossible to say.

We do not know who had interceded with King James on behalf of Lovel, but it may have been his mother-in-law, Alice, Lady Fitzhugh. This redoubtable old lady, a sister of 'Warwick the Kingmaker', was no stranger to political misfortune; and she was certainly concerned for Lovel's welfare when she wrote to her 'right trusty and welbeloved son [sic], Sir John Paston' about a 'bargane' made on her behalf at Norwich some time earlier. The first part of the letter is concerned with her own financial worries, but she then tells Paston:

'Also my doghtyr Lovell [Lady Anne Lovel] makith great sute and labour for my sone hir husbande. Sir Edwarde Franke hath bene in the North to inquire for hym; he is comyn agayne, and cane nogth understonde wher he is. Wherfore her benevolers willith hir to continue hir sute and labour; and so I can not departe nor leve hir as ye know well; and if I might be there, I wold be full glad, as knowith our Lorde God, Whoo have you in His blissid kepynge.'[13]

The letter is dated 24 February, and James Gairdner, believing it to refer to the time when Lovel 'lay concealed shortly before his outbreak with Humphrey and Thomas Stafford'[14] assigned it to 1486. The styling of Paston as 'Sir John' when, in fact, he did not receive his knighthood until after the battle of Stoke he attributed (presumably) to carelessness or unwarranted courtesy on the part of Lady Fitzhugh. Her dignifying of the unknighted Edward Frank as 'Sir Edward' would tend to support this conclusion, but if Paston *was* a knight when he received the letter then we may agree with the most recent editor of the *Letters*, the late Professor Norman Davis, that it was most probably written in February 1488.[15] It would then suggest, firstly, that Lady Anne Lovel believed, indeed knew, that her husband had survived the battle (otherwise, why make 'great sute and labour' for him); but secondly, that she had had no contact with him for a considerable period (or Edward Frank would not have been asked to inquire after him). The inference is clearly that although Lovel escaped the conflict he had disappeared by the following February. Frank 'cane nogth understonde wher he is.'[16]

One possible explanation, overlooked until Dr Gairdner rediscovered it in the public records in the last century, was that Lovel had used the interval to travel, not to Scotland (where his family and friends would have found it comparatively easy to maintain contact with him), but abroad. An inquisition post mortem dated 26 Henry VIII (i.e. 1534–5) recorded: 'They say that the same [said] Francis was overseas at the time of the predicted [i.e. laid down beforehand] attainder, and, moreover, died after the predicted [appointed] attainder [i.e. conviction], but on what day and in what year the said Francis died the appointed judges do not know.'[17]

An inquisition post mortem was 'an inquiry into the holdings, services, and succession of a deceased person who held land of the king',[18] principally to ensure that the Crown secured all the rights to which it was entitled on the death of a tenant-in-chief. It was produced, in theory, by a sworn local jury (the 'they' of the quotation), although in practice the family steward usually provided the necessary information. The source of the evidence in this case is not apparent, and since it is uncorroborated must be considered doubtful.

But it raises the question of why it was thought necessary to hold an inquiry when all Lovel's holdings had been forfeit to the Crown since Bosworth half a century earlier? There is no obvious answer, but it may have concerned the barony of Beaumont, which, under normal circumstances would have passed to Francis when his maternal uncle, William, Lord Beaumont, died childless in 1507. The issue was simply that if, on the one hand, Lovel had survived his uncle, then the barony was subject to his attainder and automatically vested in the Crown: but if, on the other hand, he had predeceased him, then the inheritance was untainted and could be called out of abeyance in favour of collateral descendants. It does not seem improbable that by the 1530s Lovel's courtier nephews, John and Henry Norris, may have been pressing Henry VIII for at least a moiety of the Beaumont properties; and a verdict which tended to favour the former possibility (by leaving the precise date of his passing open to question), would have been entirely acceptable to the King.

Indeed, even the one seemingly definite piece of information afforded by the inquiry – that Lovel was abroad 'at the time of the "predicted" attainder' – may have been designed to 'prove' that he had long survived his disappearance. The statement poses a slight difficulty in that Lovel was attainted on two occasions, the first within a few months of Bosworth (7 November 1485), and the second some ten years afterwards in October 1495. The inquisition post mortem (or, more precisely, the extract which Gairdner copied from it) does not indicate which attainder is meant; but since Lovel was in sanctuary at Colchester in the closing months of 1485 (something the jurors would surely have known of) it must be supposed that they were referring to the second indictment rather than the first. Their verdict was, apparently, that he had survived well into the last decade of the fifteenth century; and this being established, the Crown might reasonably conjecture that he had outlived Lord Beaumont too.

The passing of the second Act of Attainder is itself something of a mystery since it was apparently entirely unnecessary. The 1485 Act was comprehensive:[19] no room was left whereby its victims might suffer further disablement, and in the case of Lovel there is no evidence that it was ever reversed. The second indictment purported to attaint him on the grounds that he had been 'ignorauntly left oute and omitted'[20] from the act passed against Lincoln and the other rebels in 1487, but since he already stood convicted of high treason his inclusion then, as later, would have made no practical difference. We have already seen how the Crown appropriated Henry Lovel's properties in 1489–90, clear evidence that the earlier legislation retained its competence and could be used to deny the inheritance to other members of the family. So why did the authorities choose to omit Francis in 1487 (they could hardly have forgotten him!), and why did they suddenly decide to correct their 'error' in 1495?

The most likely answer to the first part of the question is that King Henry thought that Lovel might still be useful to him. He is not mentioned in the preamble to the attainder (which traces the course of the rebellion in some detail) and the only logical conclusion is that the government had decided to 'overlook' his part in the recent troubles as a first step towards bridging the gap between them. The King's hopes of learning the full extent of the intrigues against him from Lincoln had been dashed by the Earl's death on the battle-field,[21] but there was no reason why he could not obtain the same – and perhaps more – information from a contrite and grateful Lovel. Francis did not respond, of course – perhaps he was no longer able to – but Henry may still have hoped to lure him from hiding when he granted the 'beloved in Christ, Anne lady Lovell'[22] an annuity in December 1490. The King did not often speak endearingly of the wives of traitors, still less give them money; but the appearance of Perkin Warbeck a year later made the Simnel rebellion (and anything Lovel could have told Henry about it), increasingly irrelevant. Hopes that he would one day emerge from his hiding place would also have faded in the 1490s (whatever the Crown sought to prove in the next century), and an inquisition post mortem dated 29 October 1492 into the holdings of one John Samuell names him as one of several feoffees 'now deceased'.[23] By 1495 it must have been apparent that there was nothing left but to make him an example to other ill-disposed persons (not least, perhaps, to deny any suggestion that the Crown had once been ready to pardon him!), and his 'omission' in 1487 became the excuse for a second indictment framed for this purpose. The remark that the error had been 'to the moost perillous ensample of other being of suche traiterous myndes'[24] leaves little doubt that the Act was designed more as a warning to the present generation than as a punishment for offences long past.

But if the story that Lovel had escaped abroad was only a device to explain his disappearance to the Crown's advantage, where did the answer to the mystery really lie? Much speculation has been aroused by a letter dated 9 August 1737 written by one William Cowper, 'clerk of the Parliament', to Francis Peck, the antiquary, concerning a curious discovery made beneath the Lovel family's manor house at Minster Lovel, Oxon. Cowper recorded:

'On the 6 May 1728, the present D[uke] of R[utland] related in my hearing that, about twenty years then before (viz. in 1708, upon occasion of new laying a chimney at Minster Lovel) there was dis-covered a large vault or room under-ground, in which was the entire skeleton of a man, as having been sitting at a table, which was before him, with a book, paper, pen, etc. etc.; in another part of the room lay a cap; all much mouldred and decayed. Which the family and others judged to be this lord Lovel, whose exit hath hitherto been so uncertain.'[25]

The only other nearly contemporary account of the discovery is that published in a detailed compilation entitled *A Genealogical History of the House of Yvery* in 1742. These volumes, usually attributed to James Anderson, are principally the work of John Perceval, first Earl of Egmont, with whom Anderson collaborated as researcher and editor; and it is potentially very interesting to find the matter noticed by someone who was not only a distant kinsman of the Lovels[26] but an accomplished antiquary also. Unfortunately, however, Egmont records little with which we are not already familiar from Cowper's version of the story. There are one or two additional particulars, notably that the body was found richly clothed and remained whole until air was admitted to the chamber, but little to suggest that they are first-hand or authoritative. It is unlikely that the soft tissue of the corpse would have lasted for two centuries, and the skeleton would have collapsed as the skin, muscles and ligaments supporting it decayed. Bones are very durable, however – they can remain in good condition for several thousand years unless their surroundings are highly acidic – and it would be surprising if everything 'fell to dust'[27] when the workmen entered the chamber. The probability is that the Earl had little knowledge of these matters, and his account, with its dark allusions to neglect and treachery, appears rather to foreshadow the speculations of later writers than to provide information which may be regarded as new or genuinely helpful. We cannot even be sure that it preserves a tradition wholly independent of Cowper, since either Egmont or Anderson could have seen the abstract of the letter which Peck had printed in his *Collection of Divers Curious Historical Pieces* some two years before.[28]

But by far the most important consideration is whether, or to what extent, the report is historically accurate. It could, arguably, be regarded as merely an aberration of a similar legend concerning Sir Thomas Broughton, who was also reputed to have escaped from the battlefield and to have lived, incognito, among his tenants at Witherstack, in Westmoreland.[29] The author of the York House Books recorded that he 'fled'[30] with Lovel, and he is among those named in the 1488 Scottish safe conduct: but there is nothing to connect his survival to the circumstances peculiar to the discovery at Minster Lovel, and his story may be linked to those of other fugitives who found safety in the fastnesses of northern England. Lovel had himself sought refuge with Broughton after the failure of his 1486 rebellion, and a popular tale claimed that their enemy Lord Clifford had been concealed by his mother and brought up as a shepherd.[31] Alternatively, there may be a connection with the ancient and enigmatic ballad which attaches to the Minster Lovel ruins, the *Mistletoe Bough Chest*. This tells of how, one Christmas, when the manor was celebrating its young lord's wedding, his bride challenged the company to a game of hide and seek. She successfully concealed herself in a large chest kept, apparently, in a little-used part of the mansion, but when the time came to reveal her hiding-place found that she was unable to escape. Lord Lovel and his guests searched the house frantically, but many years passed before the trunk was noticed or someone had occasion to look inside:

> 'At length an old chest that had long lain hid,
> Was found in the castle – they raised the lid;
> And a skeleton form lay mouldering there,
> In the bridal wreath of a lady fair'[32]

These lines were written by Thomas Haynes Bayly (1797–1859), but Samuel Rogers (1762–1855) tells the story of a renaissance bride, Ginevra Orsini, and there are, or were, chests associated with the legend at Dalby Hall (Leics), Exton Hall (Rutland) and another Lovel property, Greys Court, near Henley on Thames.[33]

It would be fascinating (although perhaps ultimately unrewarding) to trace the process by which the original notice of the discovery has developed into the fine circumstantial story now found in popular literature, but Wilson MacArthur's experience is an example of what can – and sometimes does – happen. MacArthur visited Minster Lovel in 1946 while researching his book *The River Windrush*, and was regaled with a yarn which linked the discovery of the body to a search for the treasure reputedly buried with it – a search conducted by characters such as a monk named Tobias and two women 'perhaps former servants of the Lovels', Mrs Sweetbread and Mrs Littlemouse. These details were then part of the tradition, and MacArthur felt certain that 'the names alone proclaim the story true'.[34] Yet they were no more than a figment of the imagination of John Buchan, whose *The Blanket of the Dark* had been published only fifteen years earlier! It is clearly unusual that two incarceration stories should be associated with the same building, but whether they arose independently, or whether one has borrowed from, or contributed to, the other, remains uncertain. Bayly may have related the missing bride story to Minster Lovel because he heard that a body had been discovered there, but the tradition is clearly much older and could have been associated with the manor before 1708.

Yet whatever colour the intervening centuries have added to the mystery, they have afforded no substitute for the simple direct testimony of Cowper's original report. The 'clerk of the Parliament's' information was at best third-hand, but he writes soberly and reflectively, and with the conviction that he was retelling a true story. The Duke of Rutland's recollection of the discovery, or, rather, his recollection of the account of the discovery he had been given, could have been defective in some particulars, but there is a clear note of authenticity in his reference to a chimney at the manor house being re-constructed or 'new laid'. Later writers (the Earl of Egmont among them) mistakenly assumed that the remains were found when the building was demolished about 1740, but Cowper's date is consistent with his inference that it was then in a good state of repair.

The report does not, unfortunately, identify the source of the Duke's infor-mation, but it was very probably the then owner of the manor, Thomas Coke. John Manners, the future Duke of Rutland, and Coke, the future Earl of Leicester, were both Whig MPs in the 1720s, and would have met regularly in the House of Commons and when they were appointed to positions at court and in government. Coke was only eleven years old when the remains were discovered and may not have lived at Minster Lovel; but he would probably have heard the story from an eye-witness, and perhaps made further inquiries when he spent part of his honeymoon there in 1718. But whatever his interest in the matter, it is not reflected in any document preserved in the family archive at Holkham, and the Duke of Rutland's correspondence (described by his editor, H.C. Maxwell-Lyte, as 'very scanty')[35] is similarly mute. The best we can say is that Coke was well-placed to know something of the discovery, and that the time sequence – his visit to Minster Lovel in 1718 and his connections with the Duke of Rutland in the 1720s – accords well enough with the Duke retelling the story in Cowper's presence in 1728.

The evidence, then, would appear to be well-founded, but the mere fact of the discovery does not prove that the corpse was Lovel's. We must remember that the two centuries which had elapsed since his disappearance had witnessed marked political and religious upheavals, and the remains could be those of a later fugitive, a devotee of the old Catholic religion or a royalist hiding from Cromwell's troopers. Cowper himself recorded that clerkly items such as a book, a pen, and paper were found in the chamber, and there is no mention of the weapons which Lovel would surely have kept by him. But this being said, there is no reason why he should not have retired into Oxfordshire after the battle and found refuge with his former servants in the great house. Minster Lovel had been granted to the King's uncle, Jasper, Duke of Bedford, in March 1486, but he is unlikely to have visited the property, still less have resided in it, in the turbulent first years of the Tudor era. The staff, whose lives would, in many cases, have been closely bound up with the manor, would have retained their positions (at least in the interim), and would not have spurned a man who had long been their master and whose disfavour was by no means permanent. The secrecy which surrounded his concealment and its close, personal nature would have made written communication both dangerous and unnecessary, but rumours inevitably leaked into the locality and found their way into Lord Bacon's *History of the Reign of King Henry VII* published in 1622. Bacon notes the stories that Lovel may have died in the battle or drowned afterwards, swimming his horse across the river, but then adds that 'yet another report leaves him not there, but that he lived long after in a cave or vault'.[36] This report, whatever its provenance, contains no hint of a tragedy, and we are left to assume from the context that Lovel remained in his hiding place until he died naturally. But it leaves little doubt that, nearly a century before the vault was located, some dim memory of his return to Minster, unknown to the earlier chroniclers, had lingered to Bacon's day. The influence of the *Mistletoe Bough* and northern legends cannot be entirely discounted, but the story seems compelling in the light of the workmen's subsequent discovery. Coincidences may sometimes conspire to mislead us, but the balance of probability is that this is indeed where the answer to the mystery lies.

It remains then, to consider when, and under what circumstances, Lovel is most likely to have died. Again, our conclusions must necessarily be conjectural, but the probability is that the end came suddenly and without warning, and within a few months of the battle of Stoke. This is suggested by Cowper's statement that the body was found *as having been sitting* in a chair[37] (most people, when they sense death approaching, either choose or are obliged to lie down); and secondly by the perplexed tone of Lady Fitzhugh's letter, indicating that, after some initial contact with Lovel, there had been a long unexplained silence by February 1488. Francis was, moreover, a man of action, someone who would have regarded the chamber as a temporary refuge until the commotion had subsided and he could again travel more freely. There can be little doubt that, had he lived, he would have emerged to support one or another of the claimants and pretenders who continued to challenge Henry's mastery of his kingdom, and there is no evidence to support the speculation (begun, apparently, by Bacon) that he remained in his hiding place for many years.

The cause of his death must also remain uncertain, but again, there is nothing to confirm the romantic notion that something befell the servant he had entrusted with the key to his hiding place. The few details preserved by Cowper contain no hint of despair or frustration, and it would seem that death overtook him quietly and unexpectedly as he sat in his chair. Soon, probably within hours, his friends would have entered the chamber and beheld the dilemma which confronted them. Their first reaction would have been to consider how they could bury their late master with at least the minimum of religious ceremony; but commonsense would have told them that even a small private funeral would not long remain secret. Even the simple act of laying out and covering the body would have revealed their complicity to a later, perhaps less friendly, discoverer, and whatever risks they had run on their lord's behalf since his return to the manor they would clearly avail him nothing now. Perhaps, then, they removed his weapons and anything else of value, and left him as they found him. They had at least served him well in life.

And what of Lady Anne Lovel, who would have been more concerned than anyone to discover what had become of her lord? There is, unfortunately, no evidence of how long she survived his disappearance, but she was clearly still living when the second attainder was passed against him in 1495. The Act describes her as 'Anne Viscountess Lovell, late wife of the said Fraunces late Viscount Lovell'[38] suggesting again that she was then considered to be a widow; but there is no evidence that she ever remarried or acknowledged that her husband had died. She had clearly retained the royal favour noted in the granting of her annuity in 1490, for the Act was at pains to ensure that this exemplary judgement was:

> 'in noo wise prejudiciall ne hurtfull to Anne Viscountess Lovell ... to or for any Estate made of any of the premysses, to the said late Viscount and the said Anne, ne to any other psone or psones, to or for any astate made of any of the premysses, by the said late Viscount, or any other, to th'use of the said Anne: but that the same Anne, or suche other psone or psones, to whom any suche astate or astates hath ben made to th'use of the same Anne of any of the premysses, have and enjoye such pte [part] of the premysses, as any suche astate hath been made of, as they shuld have doon, if this Acte or any other Acte in this present Parliament, had never be had ne made.'[39]

It would be fascinating to know what she, of all people, made of the mystery, but in this, as in so many other curious matters, history is tantalisingly mute.

Chapter 8
A Yorkist Victory?

It has been said that history is fact, speculation is fiction, and fiction is, historically, of no value. But our lives would be poorer without fiction, or imagination, and many historical inquiries owe something to them. The battle of Stoke confirmed Henry VII on his throne and made possible the reigns of Henry VIII and Queen Elizabeth; but a Yorkist victory would have removed the nascent Tudor dynasty and Henry VIII and Elizabeth I might never have existed. We know, of course, what did happen and the rest is speculation: but English History could (arguably) have followed a very different course if 'John II' or 'Edward VI' and their successors had governed well into the sixteenth century. What that course was, and what would, or would not, then have happened may be dismissed as a flight of fancy, but at least some if it would have become reality if the verdict had gone the other way.

The first and most obvious result of such an outcome is that Bosworth would now be regarded as a temporary victory of little consequence (except, of course, for the death of King Richard), while Stoke would be seen as the critical moment when the House of York recovered the throne. The significance of one would be enhanced and the other diminished, but this is not to say that the 'last' battle of the Wars of the Roses would now be commemorated in Nottinghamshire rather than Leicestershire. Edward, Earl of Warwick was the Yorkist kings' closest male relative, but he was debarred from the succession by the attainder of his father, Clarence. This could have been set aside in Parliament or cancelled automatically by his coronation, but its continuance would have helped the Earl of Lincoln 'to seize the throne himself in the event of victory'.[1] Lincoln may have thought this both legal and appropriate since the lords were (as yet) under no obligation to accept a child who happened to be nearest in blood to a deceased ruler when another member of the royal family of full age was available.[2] He had expected to succeed his uncle, King Richard, if Richard died childless; but it unlikely that supporters of the great house of Neville would have permitted 'their' candidate to be superseded by a man who, whatever his current pretensions, was still only the great-great-great-grandson of a Hull merchant. We cannot tell if the Yorkist party would have divided against itself, either in the aftermath of Stoke or when Warwick reached maturity, but the merest hint of rivalry or disaffection would have given fresh hope to Henry Tudor. Henry would probably have retired to France after his defeat, but would have made a new bid for the crown as soon as an expedition could be organised or when the situation in England appeared favourable. His marriage to Elizabeth of York meant that he could now appeal directly to the loyalty of Edward IV's former adherents as well as to his own, more traditional, Lancastrian power base, and the result would have been a renewed conflict between two – or at worst three – 'Yorkist' factions. Stoke would clearly not have been the last battle of the Wars of the Roses, and it is difficult to see how a compromise or settlement could have been reached.

Let us assume, however, that Henry Tudor would have again been defeated and that Warwick, or more probably Lincoln, would have reigned as king. Henry might have been captured and executed, or driven into permanent exile, and this would have posed the problem of what was to be done with Elizabeth of York and her infant son, Arthur. It is likely that her marriage to Henry would have been declared invalid (probably on the grounds that he had wed her before the papal dispensation authorising a union between two persons related within the prohibited degrees of consanguinity had arrived in England), and that both she and the now 'illegitimate' Arthur would have been kept in honourable but close confinement. She might have been married to Warwick as a means of uniting two of the factions (those in power would not have scrupled to ask Rome to approve a union between first cousins when it suited them), and it is possible that she would have again reigned as queen and that one of her children would have succeeded to the throne. Lincoln already had a wife, however (Margaret Fitzalan, a daughter of the Earl of Arundel), and it is likely that under his aegis Elizabeth would have become a largely unseen and half-forgotten figure. The threat posed by her son would have waxed greater as he grew older (particularly if he established secret relations with his exiled father) and he might have ended his days as another 'Prince in the Tower'.

The new government – whatever its colour – would have had to watch, and indeed 'manage', Elizabeth of York and her offspring carefully, and the same cautions would have applied (to a lesser extent) to any children born to her four sisters. Cecily, the eldest, had been married to Ralph Scrope, a younger brother of Lord Thomas, in Richard III's reign, but the union was dissolved after Bosworth and she and her siblings, Anne (b. 1475), Catherine (b. 1479) and Bridget (b. 1480) were all single and childless in June 1487. They posed no immediate threat to their Yorkist kinsmen, but it was almost inevitable that some of them would eventually marry and produce sons – grandsons of Edward IV – who might one day challenge Lincoln's or Warwick's offspring for the throne. The obvious solution was to ensure that they remained unmarried, but this was virtually impossible short of sending them to the cloister. Elizabeth I ordered that Lady Jane Grey's two sisters, Katherine and Mary, should remain single to ensure that their claim to her throne died with them. But they both contracted clandestine unions, and neither the Queen's rage nor their long-enforced separations from their husbands prevented one of them, Katherine, from bearing two children. Wiping out a rival claim was, as even Henry VIII discovered, wholly impracticable, and only ability, firm government, and genuine popularity could secure an insecure throne.

The problems which confronted Henry Tudor at his accession were comparable with those which had taxed his late father-in-law, King Edward, a quarter of a century earlier. The battle of Bosworth had swept away King Richard's ministers in much the same way that Northampton and Towton had destroyed the governing coterie in the previous generation, and the new King was obliged to tread warily until he discovered who, beyond his immediate circle, was genuinely committed to him. His prime concern was to limit the power of the great aristocrats, to make it impossible for them to depose him as they had sometimes removed his predecessors; and it was the manner in which he achieved this which, in all probability, sets him apart from Lincoln and Warwick and from their likely attitude towards the nobility if either of them had gained power.

The demise of the 'Middle Ages', and of two of the more notorious features of late-medieval aristocratic society – bastard feudalism and the 'over-mighty' subject – are variously said to have occurred as early as the 1470s and as late as the 1530s. The late Professor Myers believed that the battles of Barnet and Tewkesbury 'opened a new period in the history of the English monarchy'.[3] Warwick's death, he argued, relieved King Edward of the menace of a 'mayor of the palace', and the Crown (which was now, thanks to royal commercial interests and French subsidies, solvent for the first time in generations) could look forward to a new era of freedom from parliamentary and lordly authority. Henry VII should not, in Myers's view, be considered the 'first of the modern kings of England; for neither in outlook, aims, nor methods did he make any important innovation, and no break with the medieval past occurred in his reign'.[4] The 'new order' of the second period of Edwardian government was, he maintained, continued by the first of the Tudors inasmuch as he quarrelled with France, allied with Spain, promoted trade agreements and the means of restoring law and order, brought his servants onto the Council to the exclusion of the magnates, recognised the wisdom of securing the support of the Pope and the ecclesiastical hierarchy, and strove after financial independence while acknowledging the need for magnificence of state. The real break with the medieval past came, Myers thought, with the Renaissance and the

Reformation, and, most profoundly, with the dissolution of the monasteries, which 'obliterated what had been one of the most prominent strands of English life for a thousand years'.[5]

There is, of course, much of value in Myers's argument, but issue must be taken with the underlying premise that 1485 (and 1487) was less significant as a turning point than the crisis of 1470–1. Between 1399 and 1485 there were ten major noble-inspired rebellions against the reigning monarch: the deposition of Richard II, the Percy and Scrope risings against his Lancastrian supplanter; the 'Southampton Plot' against Henry V; the Yorkist revolution of 1461; the 'readeption' of Henry VI and the restoration of King Edward; Richard III's usurpation; Buckingham's rebellion; and Henry Tudor's invasion. This phenomenon should, according to the various interpretations, have ended with the battle of Tewkesbury or continued down to the 1530s; but, remarkably, there were no comparable risings against the earlier Tudors after the Simnel rebellion until the Lady Jane Grey plot in 1553. Perkin Warbeck was little supported by Englishmen in general, still less by the greater families – the Cornish rising of 1497 was a popular reaction against taxation – and it was the new order of society rather than the reigning monarch which was threatened by the 'Pilgrimage of Grace'. Similarly, Wolsey concentrated more power in both Church and State into his own hands than any minister of the crown before him and exercised it in a way which was without precedent; but he commanded no private army of retainers, and his great authority evaporated when he was unceremoniously abandoned by Henry VIII.

Our hypothesis, then, is that Bosworth and Stoke marked the beginning of a new relationship between the monarch and his greatest subjects, a change which can be illustrated by comparing the ways in which Edward IV and Henry VII dealt with bastard feudalism and potentially 'over-mighty' subjects. In 1468 an Act of Parliament had extended the law restricting retaining (in effect, the recruitment of private armies) by making it illegal for the lords to sign contracts of this nature with anyone except their household servants, officials, and legal counsel. But King Edward accepted that the new restrictions should not apply to what was tacitly described as 'lawful service'; and William, Lord Hastings (our best-documented example) was able to indent on a large scale – and with royal approval – by including in his contracts such limiting phrases as 'lawful and reasonable causes', 'as right, law, and conscience requireth', and 'according to the king's laws'. Hastings, of course, remained unswervingly loyal to his royal master; but the power he accumulated *could* have been misused had he chosen otherwise. Henry VII realised that control of the magnates and their retinues was essential to the stability of his dynasty, but that mere suppression would destroy the very affinities through which the

Crown maintained order in the countryside and raised national armies as and when necessary. James Harrington's comment that a monarchy could be of two kinds 'the one by arms, the other by a nobility' and 'a monarchy, divested of its nobility, has no refuge under heaven but an army'[6] was as true of Henry as it had been true of his predecessors; and his problem, in the words of S.T. Bindoff, 'was how to suppress the magnates' abuse of power while preserving the (essential) power itself'.[7] Professor Lander has argued that the King achieved this by his reluctance to restore those attainted for treason, by at one time or another requiring no fewer than thirty-six of the sixty-two peerage families to give potentially ruinous bonds and recognisances for their own loyalty or for that of others, and by instigating an Act of Parliament which required all retinue leaders to obtain a royal licence: but Henry, overall, pardoned a slightly larger proportion of his enemies than King Edward; the numbers of bonds (which were a common feature of medieval relationships) increased only after the turn of the century, and the House of Tudor had ruled England for nearly two decades when retinues were licensed in 1504.[8] The financial penalties were, arguably, as much a reflection of the King's avariciousness as of a desire to control the nobility, and the magnates' meek compliance suggests that this was the culmination, rather than the beginning, of a process of limitation which had formed part of his policy for many years.[9]

The truth of the matter is that King Henry's subjection of his nobility had begun soon after his accession; long, in fact, before he had overcome the various challenges to his authority, and employed a strategy which may be summed up in the phrase 'divide and rule'. He was bound to restore vanquished Lancastrians to some of their former holdings, but could not entirely dispossess those Yorkists who had held Lancastrian properties and had been loyal to the Crown for a quarter of a century. The resulting compromise allowed him to give something to many rather than much to fewer, and meant that peers who had enjoyed vice-regal authority in particular regions found themselves restricted by the return of old rivals. Edward Hastings, for example, was obliged to surrender estates in Leicestershire and Lincolnshire to Lords Roos and Beaumont, and although he subsequently leased back some of the manors restored to Beaumont he never regained the influence and status enjoyed by his father, executed by Richard III in 1483.[10] It could be argued that Henry was responding to circumstances rather than pursuing a 'policy'; but it is significant that some lords who had kept a foot in both camps or whose holdings were not partially resumed still found themselves increasingly side-lined. Lord Stanley, Henry's stepfather, was rewarded with some of Francis Lovel's forfeited estates besides those of the Harringtons and, as we have seen, given the title Earl of Derby; but his seat at Lathom in Lancashire diminished as a centre of regional government under his step-son's aegis, and he lost much of his influence after 1485. It is likely that when Henry obliged men like Stanley and Northumberland to collect harsher taxes he was aware that he was diminishing their popularity with their 'well-wishers'; and Dr Cunningham has suggested that he sensed the irony of making some lesser figures who were pardoned and restored to their former positions after Stoke collect money from the same people they had only recently urged to rebel against him![11] They were also required to find sureties who would guarantee their behaviour in future, and turned, inevitably, to other former supporters of Richard III who had not offended Henry but who now faced financial ruin if their erstwhile colleagues were again tempted to flirt with treason. King Edward was prepared to place unwarranted power in the hands of William Hastings because he trusted him implicitly; but Henry Tudor, although 'made' a king, trusted no one with the means of kingmaking. He did not seek to suppress the nobility because they, as a class, were essential to the maintenance of public order and the defence of the kingdom. Rather, he controlled them, not with bonds and recognisances (which, though a deterrent, could be cancelled by a determined and victorious rebel) nor by legislation and licences (which were imposed only after he had created the conditions necessary for their acceptance), but by diversifying lands and offices, the basis of their authority, so that whatever their overt or covert intentions they would always lack the financial wherewithal to recruit a dangerously large following. He believed, Vergil wrote, that 'whenever they (his subjects) gave him offence they were actuated by their great wealth' and determined to deprive them of their fortunes so that they should be 'less well able to undertake any upheaval';[12] and Henry VIII (who had clearly learned much from his father) 'graciously remarked that he had an evil people to rule and promised that he would make them so poor that they would never be able to rebel again'.[13] It is unlikely that this would have happened under a Yorkist administration since there would have been no permanent restoration of former Lancastrians nor, probably, would Warwick or Lincoln have thought in terms of fundamentally changing Edward IV's policies. Baronial authority, with its tendency towards lawlessness, would have continued well into the sixteenth century, and the 'Middle Ages' would have lasted significantly longer in this respect.

A second sea-change which occurred under the Tudors – the break with Rome and the dissolution of the monasteries – might also not have happened if the Yorkists had won at Stoke. Henry VIII was a traditionalist in outlook, devout, orthodox, respectful of, and respected by, the papacy which in 1521 granted him the title Defender of the Faith in response to the dedication of his book denouncing Luther. Heresy, in the form of Lollardy, was confined to the major urban centres and attracted few besides obscure and humble people; and in a country where a measure of royal authority in the Church (most notably the King's right to appoint bishops), was now accepted by the papacy, there seemed no reason why the consensus should be seriously shaken. There were bound to be occasions when the Church which, through its courts, claimed authority over all matters of faith and morals (in a very wide sense) and the right to try nearly all literates, would find itself at odds with the monarchy; but the two sides had always been reconciled, even after events such the murder of Thomas Becket and Henry IV's execution of Archbishop Scrope. So why was it in Henry's reign (and not in any other) that the Church in England was 'revolutionised, humbled and despoiled'?[14]

The immediate cause of the breach with Rome was Henry's wish to divorce Catherine of Aragon, but this no more answers our question than the equally sweeping statement that the Church was in need of reform. True, non-residence and pluralism were growing rather worse in the early sixteenth century (Wolsey, for example, held the wealthiest bishopric, Winchester, and the richest abbey, St Albans, besides his archbishopric of York), but it is arguable that corruption had reached even greater heights during the Avignon papacy without the Church–State relationship in England being seriously threatened. There was, however, a new factor emerging – the growth of nationalism as opposed to internationalism, that is, the old concept of belonging to the whole of Christendom. The popes were increasingly seen as Italian princes who drained English resources for purposes which were of no concern to England, and there were those who, like Bishop Gardiner, thought it possible and desirable to be independent of the papacy without opening the door to Protestantism. The monasteries, who valued their direct links with the papacy and their freedom from ecclesiastical authority, were almost bound to find themselves on the wrong side of this argument, and although the monks were mostly Englishmen they were increasingly regarded as an alien element in the English Church. A century of royal and episcopal efforts to reform the now-degenerate orders had proved unsuccessful, and a critical generation was forming the opinion that their great resources could be better used elsewhere.

These factors alone would have been enough to justify calls for reform of the Church in England, and there were others which made it seem less relevant to contemporaries than it had to their medieval ancestors. It no longer enjoyed a monopoly of learning by the early sixteenth century, and stood for a per-manence in the ordering of society which was increasingly outmoded. The rising merchant class adhered to principles of self-reliance and progress which chimed ill with the Church's teaching on such matters as usury; and many townsmen, far from being illiterate, were often better educated than their poorly paid parish priests. The invention of printing meant that people were no longer dependent on cloister and pulpit for information, and the new middle-class household began to replace the Church as the centre of social life in the community. Merchants were influenced by Lutheran teachings they heard on the Continent, and soon the Bible was being unofficially translated into English. The clergy might have led the way in this development, but they were too afraid for their own authority to do so. As Canon Maynard Smith once commented, 'the theologians no more encouraged the laity to read scripture than a modern solicitor encourages his clients to read *Every Man His Own Lawyer*'!

But perhaps the single most important factor in the downfall of papal authority in England was, ironically, Cardinal Wolsey. It seems almost unthinkable that this great churchman who aspired to become pope should have contributed to the break with the old order; but he concentrated so much power in the Church in England in his own person that Henry VIII could be forgiven for thinking that if such dominance could be exercised by the son of an Ipswich butcher, then why not by the King himself? Wolsey, as legate, asserted his authority over the religious as well as the secular clergy, and his arbitrary dissolution of a score of monastic houses to finance his educational ambitions showed Henry how he could replenish his own empty treasury. It is no exaggeration to say that the Cardinal established an unprecedented autocracy, and that it was he, and not his royal master, who first exceeded the accepted precedents of what could – or could not – be done with the Church in England. Wolsey was the last of the great clerical chancellors, and the break with the past is nowhere better emphasised than in the transfer of authority to the first of the great layman-secretaries, Thomas Cromwell, who would henceforth be the chief ministers of the Crown.

Henry VIII seems to have entertained the belief that Wolsey was the main obstacle to his divorce from Catherine of Aragon, but the Pope, predictably, proved no more amenable after his downfall. The theologians of the great universities of Europe were asked to confirm that the Mosaic law which forbade marriage with a deceased brother's widow could not be overridden by a papal dispensation, and the King, fortified by the knowledge that he had always been a bachelor, began to make his own solution on his own terms. Henry, for his part, saw himself as a conservative reformer who had purged the English Church of its abuses while retaining its catholic traditions; but the abolition of papal authority and the dissolution of the monasteries were revolutionary changes, and were bound ultimately to lead to more. His use of Parliament to sanction his reforms greatly increased the competence and standing of the Commons; and the redistribution of perhaps one-sixth of all the land in

England gave the rising middle classes an unprecedented opportunity to acquire estates and properties. The Reformation was not therefore merely an ecclesiastical matter, but profoundly affected the ordering of society too.

It follows that if Henry VIII had not become king there would have been no divorce from Queen Catherine and no bitter and dramatic rejection of papal authority. But it is likely that the Pope's influence would have diminished in the sixteenth century as the institution he headed appeared less relevant and as more Englishmen espoused Protestantism. Similarly, it is improbable that the monasteries would have been entirely destroyed if Warwick or Lincoln or their successors had determined their future; but the smaller, poorer, houses were already struggling and would probably have foundered or been obliged to amalgamate.[15] Change, therefore, there would have been, but it would have formed part of a gradual, perhaps almost imperceptible, process, which would only have been apparent with hindsight. It is impossible to know how long a resurgent Yorkist dynasty would have lasted or what its kings would have done that the Tudors did not do; but it may be worth reflecting that the Stuarts would not have become rulers of England (unless another princess had married into the royal House of Scotland and the royal line had still died out in England), and there would have been no English Civil War. Parliament, and the middle classes generally, would have continued to grow in authority, but there is no reason to suppose that there would have been a revolution in the middle of the seventeenth century or that a member of the Commons would have become head of state. It is, of course, possible that worse misfortunes would have been visited on England if the rivalry between the several 'Yorkist' claimants had continued, and if the 'Wars of the Roses' had been fought into an unknown future. Henry VII's victory at Stoke may not have been an unmixed blessing for his countrymen, but the alternatives, like Churchill's alternatives to democracy, were arguably, all potentially worse.

Chapter 9

The Battlefield Today

Note: the maps in this book display some modern features, but are designed principally to show the battlefield as it was in 1487. Visitors may find it useful to equip themselves with a copy of Ordnance Survey map Explorer 271 if they wish to walk, or drive, in the area. There are currently no facilities in East Stoke (the Paunceforte Arms is now an Indian restaurant which is only open in the evenings), but the garden centre just inside the road to Hawton has a coffee shop which closes at 4 pm (4.30 pm on Saturdays), and food is available all day at the Lord Ted pub, just past the traffic island two and three-quarter miles from Stoke on the Newark road.

The motorists who today drive along the busy Fosse Way (A46) in the direction of Newark or Leicester pass through East Stoke in a few seconds, and most, it is reasonable to assume, scarcely notice it. There are no signs either commemorating or pointing the way to the battlefield, and the information panels which briefly adorned the area when the quincentenary of the battle was celebrated in 1987 are now in retirement at the west end of St Oswald's church. Much of the area fought over is private farmland which can be viewed only from the fringes, or perimeter; but in this respect it is not unlike Bosworth and it is still possible to see most, if not quite all, of the principal features. This survey will take the form of a walking tour keeping mainly to roads or designated footpaths, and will mention possible stops at particular vantage points for those who prefer to explore the area more rapidly, or less energetically, by car.

On approaching the crossroads at the centre of Stoke village turn into Church Lane and park on your left near Humber Lane. Return to the crossroads on foot, cross to the opposite side of the A46, and turn right, following the footpath in a southerly direction. The A46 is extremely busy, so particular care is needed. Notice the 'East Stoke' sign as you pass by it on the opposite side of the road. It was some ten yards south of this that human remains believed to date from the battle were discovered in 1982. Turn left into Elston Lane, pass a modern bungalow on your left, and then look for the spring known as Willow Rundle (or Willow Runnel) where a modern spout and basin project from the bank by the roadside approximately 50 yards further on to your right. A number of battlefields – Evesham and Bosworth are examples – have watering holes where the fallen leader slaked his thirst for the last time and Stoke Field is no exception. Where you are standing was perhaps 400 yards behind the extreme left of the rebel position, and although this part of the field was not actually fought over there are two legends which connect it with the ensuing rout. One is that a dying soldier prayed to his patron saint for water and immediately, water gushed from the nearby bank; another is that Lincoln and Schwartz were buried in the immediate vicinity and that willow stakes were driven through their bodies. R.P. Shilton noted two ancient willow trees which were 'supposed to have proceeded from those stakes'[1] when he studied the area in 1827, but no trace of them remains now.

After visiting Willow Rundle retrace your steps back along Elston Lane to the A46 and turn left. Continue along the A46 until you reach Lodge Lane on your left (taking great care since it is now necessary to walk on the grass verge), cross the road, and proceed up Trent Lane (You can avoid this busy stretch of the A46 by continuing along Elston lane towards Elston, turning right at the village, and then right again into Lodge Lane, but it adds considerably to the distance). As you proceed along Trent Lane you are walking close to the position occupied by the Earl of Oxford's contingent of which the right wing, commanded by Sir Edward Woodville, would have extended to about the 35 m contour, while the left, under Sir John Savage, dominated the higher ground in the distance towards the river. The rebel army was stationed on the ridge to your right, and extended from Burham Hill in the west to approximately the 30 m contour in Elston fields to the east. Lincoln's forces advanced over the fields to engage their enemies, and the first desperate clash of the battle, with pikes and bills striking shields, and guns being fired at almost point-blank range, occurred where you are now standing. Keep your eyes open for anything which resembles shot or an arrowhead and report all finds to the County Archaeologist. It may not be likely, but you never know!

When you reach the higher ground the lane bears slightly to the right and descends towards the river. Turn right at the waymarker post, and follow the grassy path keeping the river on your left. After about 80 yards pass through a gap in the hedge and turn sharp right towards the southern end of Stoke Wood keeping the hedge on your right. (The public footpath marked on the Explorer map runs diagonally across the field in front of you, but it cannot be located on the ground). When you reach the corner of the field, turn left and follow the edge of the wood for approximately 700 yards until you come to a narrow defile in the trees on your right, just before a downward slope in the path. This is the 'Red Gutter', usually thought to be so called because it ran red with the blood of fugitive rebels caught by Oxford's men as they scrambled down it in a desperate attempt to reach the river. There can be little doubt that some did die here in this manner, but the 'Gutter' may also take its name from the red Keuper Marl clay which has been extracted from it since the Roman era. It was briefly opened to the public, with wooden 'steps' installed, in 1987, but is wholly inaccessible now.

High above and behind you to your right on Burham Hill (which, unfortunately, is private property), a small marker stands at the side of a hedgerow. This is the Burrand Bush stone, and bears the legend 'Here stood the Burrand Bush planted on the spot where Henry VII placed his standard after the battle of Stoke June 16th 1487.' R.P. Shilton says that in his time (1828) 'a large, lofty and ancient thorn tree which has borne the appellation of Burham Bush from time immemorial'[2] stood here, but it had presumably died when the Newark Archaeological and Local History Society donated the stone. The names 'Burham' and 'Burrand' were presumably interchangeable, and there is no indication of whether the flag was left on the hill for a time or was one of those presented to the church at Newark or sent to Walsingham. All we can say is that Henry's army had fought under three standards at Bosworth, one displaying the image or arms of St George, another a 'fiery' red dragon painted on white and green sarcenet, and the third a dun cow on a background of yellow *tartaryn*, a rich silken material, and it would have been possible to leave one on Stoke battlefield and still give the other two as thanks-offerings if the same pattern was followed in 1487.

Continue along the path for a short distance after leaving the Red Gutter until it joins a straight metalled track to your left. This leads to the bank of the Trent opposite Fiskerton where the rebels forded the river on their way to the battlefield and (in a few cases), made good their escape afterwards. The distance from here to the riverbank is approximately three-quarters of a mile, so unless you are particularly energetic it may be preferable to drive along this part of the route after completing the rest of the walk and returning to your car. R.P. Shilton remarks that

> 'at this season of the year the River is fordable by men, teams and cattle; and so very shallow was the water in the Summer of 1825, that on the first of August, boys not exceeding ten years of age, passed and repassed in perfect safety. And on the 20th June, 1826, the River at this place measured 47½ yards in width and 21 inches in depth.'[3]

The expanse obviously varied since Richard Brooke, who visited the battlefield in June 1823, June 1824, August 1825 and September 1827, says that the distance between the banks 'as far as I could judge by the eye, is thereabouts 160 or 180 yards wide'.[4] But he was in no doubt that horses and men could still have crossed over in safety, unlike today when the Trent appears deep and fast flowing. There was a ferry here in later times, but it has long since fallen into disuse.

If you decide to follow the metalled track to the bank of the Trent from this point, return by the same route and continue along the road which bears uphill to your right. You are now approaching the western end of the medieval village of Stoke (Stoches), and will shortly come to the high wall of St Oswald's church-yard, which you enter by a gate on your left. There is a fine bronze memorial to Julian, Baron Paunceforte, Britain's first ambassador to Washington, adjacent to the west end of the fourteenth-century tower, and a stone erected in 1987 commemorating 'John de la Pole, Earl of Lincoln, Sir Thomas Geraldine, Col. Martin Schwartz and 7,000 others, English Irish and German' facing south. It is said that some of the stones in the porch were scarred when soldiers sharpened their weapons on them before the battle, but this story is told of other places (St Margaret's, Stoke Golding, near Bosworth, for example), and is more probably where generations of sextons have sharpened their scythes.

The small church was substantially remodelled in 1738 and is not now as the combatants of 1487 would have seen it, but the chancel has late-fourteenth-century straight-headed windows with ogee tracery, while the tower arch still boasts a pair of finely moulded thirteenth-century capitals. There is a medieval piscina and some fragments of what may be fifteenth-century stained glass in the tracery lights of the south-west chancel window, but on our visit there was no sign of the old chest believed to date from the thirteenth century mentioned by both Sir Nikolaus Pevsner and Arthur Mee. The information boards which were placed around the battlefield when the quincentenary was marked in 1987 are now grouped together beneath the tower, but the flags used in the re-enactment which were hung near the west end at the conclusion of the festivities have since been removed. Frank Cotton recounts that when his father was vicar in the early part of the last century the installation of some new central-heating apparatus led to the discovery of a number of skeletons 'at a depth much below the level of present interment'.[5] It was said at the time that they were the bones of young men with well-preserved teeth, but whether they were victims of the battle or of one of the plagues which devastated the village is uncertain. The parish registers, which date from 1539, state that 159 of 161 residents who died in the year 1646 were plague victims, and interestingly, that some of them were buried in 'ye fielde'.

Stoke Hall may be glimpsed from the eastern end of the churchyard but is privately owned and not open to visitors. The present building dates from the mid-sixteenth century, although it was much reduced in size when the three-story entrance block was demolished in 1921–3. Pevsner noted some older materials which had formed part of the medieval house when he surveyed it for *The Buildings of England* and mentions particularly two early-medieval carved figures and a much weathered statue of St Leonard under a canopy. A hospital, or almshouse, dedicated to St Leonard and founded before 1135 by the Aincurt family of Thurgaton stood nearby, and a house on this site was connected to the Hall when the latter was enlarged in 1812. Francis Lovel had succeeded his grandmother, Alice, Lady Deincourt, as patron of the hospital, and it passed to the Crown after he was attainted. It was closed by Edward VI in 1548, re-founded by Philip and Mary ten years later, and finally dissolved by Queen Elizabeth in 1573. It held four messuages, nine cottages, and 177 acres, but seldom seems to have consisted of more than a master, two brethren, and the few sick or elderly residents for whom they cared.

On leaving the churchyard, turn left passing under a brick arch and make your way back towards the crossroads pausing at a gate on your right. The mounds and hollows still visible in the fields are some remains of the medieval village which once had a population of *c.* 800, far greater than in more modern times. You can now return to your car or extend the walk by turning right into Humber Lane, just after the long brick wall on the left comes to an end. This metalled lane, which soon becomes an enclosed track, formed part of the Roman 'Upper Fosse', and linked the fort of Margidunum with the bridging station at Ad Pontem (just north of Stoke village), prior to the construction of the Fosse Way in the second century AD. It was used as a drovers' road along which sheep and cattle were shepherded or herded from grazing areas to market (the deep path, formed by the animals moving closely together, is known as a 'hollowgate') and leads up to the high ground occupied by the Yorkist forces. The public right of way ends where the route continues into open fields (and where a path to the right leads towards Stoke Wood), but the rear of the rebel position is clearly defined against the skyline. The Fosse Way is in the valley to your left, while the trees mask the steep slopes to the Trent on your right. Lincoln had chosen a secure situation with broad views over the country to the south.

Those who wish to tour the battlefield by car in easy stages may stop with care near Humber Lane (as for the walking tour), next to the Church wall, and by Willow Rundle on Elston Lane. There is also some hard-standing where Church Lane joins the modern straight road leading to the Trent opposite Fiskerton, from where it is only a short walk to the lower end of the Red Gutter. The best place from which to see the battlefield as a whole is from the lay-by on the *western* side of the A46 between Elston Lane and Lodge Lane, the southern turn to Elston village. To your right, to the north-west, is the ridge occupied by the rebels before the battle (marked by a line of trees), and to your left is Trent Lane (the entrance to which is just visible from where you are standing), where the Earl of Oxford took up his position and where the two armies clashed. Lincoln's men would have passed both in front of and behind you as they advanced to battle on that fateful day in 1487.

There are two other locations which have been associated with the conflict, although neither has any firm evidence to commend it. 'Dead Man's Field', which was known to Cornelius Brown and other older historians of the county, lies in the northern angle of the A46 and the minor road to Thorpe village, but there is no record of the remains which were (presumably) found there. There is also a tradition – it can be no more than that in the circumstances – that Henry VII watched the battle from the tower of Hawton church. The tower is visible across the fields to the north-east of Burham Hill, but it is unlikely that Henry would have chosen a position well beyond the front line of his own army or risked being trapped inside by a sudden Yorkist attack. The interior of the church contains some magnificent examples of the art of the medieval stone-mason and is well worth a visit; but it is unlikely to have featured in the battle itself.

And what of the future? There are more features, both natural and man-made, to see at Stoke than exist on many English battlefields, and the arrangements made for the 1987 quincentenary showed that a trail which did not disrupt local farming could be established at the heart of the area. A plot of land or an existing building would need to be purchased to serve as an interpretative centre complete with refreshments and toilet and parking facilities, but would the villagers welcome it? As always, there would be a conflict between the economic benefits of tourism and the effects it would have on the local environment. What is needed is both the will and the money to undertake the necessary development, and this would inevitably be governed by estimates of how many visitors it would attract. Stoke, unlike Bosworth, did not usher in a new dynasty, but it could still be promoted as 'the last battle of the Wars of the Roses' and 'the last pitched battle fought on English soil in the Middle Ages'. At the time of writing (July 2005) there are plans to by-pass the village by re-routing the A46 to the south-east. The proposed works are presently outside the battlefield area as designated by English Heritage, but there is the possibility of encountering further burial pits depending on where exactly the route comes back 'on-line' with the existing road. The project is still in its early stages, but when completed it will clearly reduce the number of cars passing through the village and make the area much safer for walkers. Nottinghamshire has always lagged behind Leicestershire in the development of its premier battlefield – is now the time to consider catching up?

Chapter 10
How Do We Know?

Our knowledge of the campaigns and battles of the Wars of the Roses is patchy and limited, and this, as we have seen, is as true of Stoke as it is of more famous conflicts. Only at Towton has a mass grave of the slain yielded substantial tangible evidence, and for the rest we are forced to rely on accounts written from various standpoints and with varying degrees of competence. Our task is to winnow through the available records, compare them where possible, and construct a version of events which may not be accurate in every detail but which can claim to be the facts of the matter as far as we know them. Choices are inevitable, and this chapter will seek to explain why, sometimes, the views of one writer have been preferred to others and why we must occasionally take most, or even all, of them with a large pinch of salt.

Medieval writers did not necessarily set out to mislead their readers, but they were fanciful and apt to think that telling a good story was more important than telling a strictly accurate one. Most numbers quoted, particularly the numbers of men who fought in battles, are wildly exaggerated, and were designed more to emphasise the magnitude of a victory or excuse a disaster than to record the true size of the armies. Similarly, we might suppose that an author who was present at a battle, or was engaged in it, would be an unimpeachable authority, but this is by no means certain. A commander overlooking the scene could, possibly, write a comprehensive account of the action; but an individual soldier would know little more than what was happening in the small area of the battlefield in which he happened to be fighting. We need to consider not only the prejudices of our authorities but the intellectual milieu in which they reported and what they themselves were trying to achieve.

The first broad category of evidence available to us is derived from official records – more specifically from Acts of Parliament, royal proclamations, documents produced by the Chancery and Exchequer, and, in a northern context, the House Books of the City of York. The most useful Parliamentary Act is, of course, that passed against the Earl of Lincoln and his principal associates in 1487, supplemented by information gleaned from the indictment of Richard III's supporters after Bosworth and the attainder of Francis Lovel in 1495. Both the 1487 and 1495 Acts provide useful background information (inasmuch as they were obliged to explain why the person, or persons, named were being convicted of high treason), and tell us precisely who was held to be responsible for the uprising. The Rolls of Parliament (*Rotuli Parliamentorum*) were published in six volumes as long ago as 1767–77, and a modern scholarly edition became available in 2005.

The King's own thinking, the fears and threats which most concerned him, can be glimpsed in the proclamations he issued in the weeks immediately prior to the battle. These public ordinances 'issued by the King in virtue of his royal prerogative, with the advice of his council, under the Great Seal, and by royal writ'[1] are concerned mainly with enforcing public order, both in his own army and in the realm generally, and reveal Henry for what he then was – a new ruler, unknown to, and unsure of, the majority of his subjects. They usually prescribed dire penalties (death for theft or picking a quarrel, for example), but it is unclear how widely they were disseminated or whether those who read or heard them chose to obey them. We have seen that they did not discourage numbers of 'harlatts and vagabonds' from disturbing the peace of the army in the early stages of its march to Nottinghamshire, and so may have been similarly disregarded further afield.

Royal proclamations were entered on the dorse of the patent roll after they had passed the Great Seal, and the same source provides us with much useful information concerning the government's dealings with its greater subjects. The printed *Calendars* produced by the Public Record Office record fines, grants and pardons, and are usefully supplemented by the Reverend William Campbell's *Materials for a History of the Reign of Henry VII* in the older Rolls Series. Bonds and recognisances (suspended penalties designed to ensure the good behaviour of officeholders and those under suspicion), are recorded in

Engraving of the Great Seal of Henry VII, by Francis Sandford (1677).

the printed *Calendar of Close Rolls* and in other unpublished chancery and exchequer memoranda, and indicate the degree of trust which existed between the King and some of his more prominent subjects. It is important to remember that these documents were produced for the benefit of contemporaries, not modern historians; but they deal in hard facts as opposed to speculation and, interpreted correctly, are among the surest indicators of what really took place.

The York House Books are not, strictly speaking, minute books inasmuch as they are not a complete record of business transacted at meetings of the City Council; but the clerk invariably preserved copies of important letters and described the visits of kings and other notable persons. The Council consisted of a mayor elected from among twelve aldermen together with eighteen more junior representatives (prosaically known as the 'Twenty-Four'), three (or sometimes four) chamberlains who supervised internal finances, and two sheriffs who dealt with financial obligations to the Crown. They were supported by two professional officers, the recorder, who was usually a lawyer and who sometimes served as the City's parliamentary representative; and the common clerk, or 'secretarie' who supervised the administration and was responsible for the compilation and safe-keeping of the Books themselves. Successive clerks deposited records which had passed their immediate usefulness in a damp chamber on Ouse Bridge, where they could be consulted and from where they were sometimes borrowed by authorised persons – although whether they returned them is another matter. In 1738 they were transferred to a poorly ventilated closet in the fifteenth-century Guildhall, where they continued to deteriorate and where they suffered additional damage when the Ouse flooded in 1892. This led to belated efforts to conserve them although some of the methods employed – particularly that of sticking tissue paper to fragile leaves – only created more difficulties for future researchers. The tissue or the adhesive darkened over the years making the writing difficult to decipher, and when it was removed towards the end of the last century some of the text of the affected documents was entirely lost. Some of the ink is now very pale, and Lorraine Attreed noticed further instances of deterioration between making her original transcription of the Books in the late 1970s and preparing them for publication a decade later. There is, she considers, 'the possibility that the records will soon literally fade away'.

The first serious examination of the archive was undertaken by Darcy Preston in 1699, twenty years before he became York's town clerk. His efforts to have them moved to a properly constructed repository came to nothing, but the notes he made give some indication of subsequent losses and attempts at re-organisation.[2] Clerk Robert Davies was shocked by the state of some of the documents when he examined them in 1831, and although he too failed to persuade the authorities to build a permanent record office he was at least able to have the medieval papers placed in a fireproof safe. Francis Drake printed a selection from the Books and other miscellaneous items in 1736 (*Eboracum, or the History and Antiquities of the City of York*); but he was more concerned to illustrate his history than to make the records available to scholars. Credit for this must again go to Robert Davies, whose *Extracts from the Municipal Records of the City of York During the Reigns of Edward IV, Edward V, and Richard III* reprinted some of Drake's selections 'following the abbreviations and other peculiarities of the originals with greater exactness than was thought necessary at the time of Mr Drake's publication'[3] together with others of his own choosing. Angelo Raine edited eight volumes of selections from the first thirty surviving Books between 1939 and 1953 (*York Civic Records*), and these became a 'standard' text for half a century. But only scholars with direct access to the archive would have been aware that he had omitted many Latin documents, 'incorrectly transcribed many of the English entries, and insisted in error that some entries were missing when he had only to turn over a folio to find them.'[4] Fortunately, a full and accurate transcription of the first six Books edited by Professor Attreed was published by The Richard III and Yorkist History Trust in 1991, and these cover the period of the Simnel rebellion. There are a few entries of interest in Book Seven, most notably the arrest of the 'sympill and pure person' who claimed to have met Lord Lovel in Scotland, together with the graphic statement that Richard III 'was an ypocryte, a croche bake, and beried in a dike like a dogge', and it is still necessary to refer to the second volume of Raine's work for these.[5]

The documents which cast light on the Simnel rebellion begin with James Taite's report of the Earl of Lincoln's treason dated 31 March 1487, copies of which were sent to both the Earl of Northumberland and the Bishop of Exeter, the King's secretary. Northumberland replied that he had received a letter from the King the previous day appraising him of Lincoln's departure, and advised the citizens to be ready to subdue 'all ryot and riotous langage by any persone committed contrary to the well (being) of our souverain lord'. The mayor again wrote to King Henry on 23 April warning him that the city's defences were in a poor state of repair (partly because Richard III had failed to rebuild the demolished castle), and that there was a serious shortage of man-power. A similar, shorter, missive was also sent to Lord Chancellor Morton asking him to 'stand our good lord' with the King if John Vavasour, the recorder and bearer of the letters, failed to gain access to Henry: but Henry replied thanking the citizens for their loyalty on 28 April. Vavasour reported three days later that guns were to be sent to York from Scarborough Castle, and that Sir Richard Tunstall and six other knights had been instructed to assist the citizens 'in caas that the kinges ennymees approche thiddre'. He had, he said, been careful to ensure that these men would be under mayoral authority while they were in York in accordance with the city's ancient 'fraunchesse and liberties', because 'the maier . . . is the kinges liuetenaunt ther and (has) the chefe guyding undre the king'.

Vavasour need not have feared, however. Henry wrote on 8 May to advise the citizens that Lincoln and his forces had sailed westwards to Ireland, and he had accordingly allowed Tunstall and the others to return home for the time being. His letter was read in the Guildhall on 15 May, just one day after the Mayor had written to him at Kenilworth to complain that the promised guns from Scarborough had not arrived. There now ensued a period of some three weeks of enforced waiting until a letter dated 6 June from the Earl of Northumberland informed the citizens that the rebels had landed at Furness two days earlier. Northumberland expressed the hope that he would arrive in York by the following Sunday (10 June), but in the meantime the mayor and his brethren had to deal with Simnel's letter from Masham which arrived on Friday the 8th. They curtly refused the rebels' request for access to the city and were doubtless relieved to learn that Lincoln had decided not to force the issue. The record concludes with a narrative account of subsequent events, viz: the arrival and departure of Lord Clifford, the 'battle' of Bramham Moor, Clifford's return and second exit with Northumberland, and the return of both lords after the Scropes had attacked Bootham Bar. A servant of the recorder brought word of the royal victory on Sunday 17 June (he presumably provided the brief account of the action which was incorporated into the House Books), and the mayor ordered thanks to be given in the Minster without delay.[6]

The York House Books provide a unique, first-hand insight into some of the more northerly aspects of the Simnel rebellion, and bear comparison with the detailed, contemporary account of the royal campaign written by the herald or pursuivant who accompanied the Tudor army. This forms part of a longer narrative of events at court extending, with short interruptions, from the early months of 1486 to the beginning of 1490, and is today British Library, Cotton MS. Julius B.XII. Unfortunately, we know nothing of the author – even his name is lost to us – but it is apparent that he was close to the King throughout the weeks leading to the battle and a most acute observer of everything which occurred. His account was not a propaganda exercise – he was as ready to record Henry's difficulties as his successes – nor was he overly concerned with precedent. Rather, he appears to have set out to provide a permanent record of a series of events in which he participated and which he thought might prove to be of significance. He seems to have been better informed than other writers – no one else, apparently, was aware that Simnel's real name was 'John'; and the only disappointment is that he did not witness the actual battle. It is likely that he and other non-combatants were stationed a safe distance from the fighting, and he knew only that Lincoln had been slain, Simnel captured, and Lovel vanquished. Perhaps he was proud of his eye-witness testimony and reluctant to allow second-hand recollections to corrupt it: but, equally, he was primarily concerned with the King's activities, and Henry's caution in the face of danger may have left him with little more to say.

More distant in time, although still closely contemporary, is the account of the rebellion given by Polydore Vergil. Vergil was born in Urbino, in Italy, about 1470, and came to England when his patron, Adriano Castelli, was appointed Bishop of Hereford in 1502. He was already a noted author, and this is probably why Henry VII asked him to write a new history of England, in Vergil's words, to 'display eternally to the living those events which should be an example and those which should be a warning.'[7] He had completed his researches and a first draft by 1513, and simultaneously helped Castelli promote England's interests at the papal court in Rome. He was rewarded with the archdeaconry of Wells (1508), and his career prospered mightily until he and his patron fell foul of Wolsey. He spent some months in prison in 1515, and thereafter devoted himself to his religious duties and to literature, producing, among other works, an edition of Gildas and the first printed version of the *Anglica Historia* in 1534. He duly signed the denial of papal supremacy, played a formal part Henry VIII's divorce of Anne of Cleves, and composed a letter congratulating Queen Mary on her accession shortly before returning to reside in Urbino, where he died in April 1555.

Vergil was a conscientious historian who had access both to official documents and to eye-witness testimony, but his account of events leading to the battle is disappointing in several respects. He was surely naive in believing that the conspiracy was wholly the brainchild of the priest Simons (who, he says, convinced Sir Thomas Geraldine, who sold the story to the Irish nobility, who then drew in Margaret of Burgundy and the Earl of Lincoln); and misunderstands the manoeuvrings of the armies in the twenty-four hours before the engagement. It is possible that he had some difficulty understanding what Englishmen said to him (his grasp of the vernacular may have been far from perfect even after ten years in the country), and that he relied heavily on what he was told by fellow Latin-speaking clergymen whose knowledge of the campaign, and particularly the battle, was at best second-hand. One of his informants was undoubtedly Christopher Urswick, who features more prominently in Vergil's version of the story than in any other. Urswick brought word of the rebels' landing to the King and subsequently carried his standard to Walsingham as a thanks-offering: but his contribution to Henry's victory was probably less than that of others who are hardly noticed. Vergil may even be guilty of deliberate deception inasmuch as he gives an altogether implausible reason for the incarceration of Elizabeth Woodville, and there can be no doubt that his over-riding purpose was, in Denys Hay's words, 'to put a favourable interpretation on the rise of the House of Tudor'.[8] He is an essential source for the Simnel uprising, but may not always have told (or been able to tell), the whole truth.

Another interesting, if somewhat perplexing, source of information is the chronicle of Jean Molinet. Molinet was historiographer to the ducal house of Burgundy before becoming librarian to Margaret of Austria, Charles the Bold's granddaughter, and his narrative extends from 1474 to the year before he died in 1507. Contemporaries thought him a better poet than historian, and one modern commentator has described his literary style as a 'ridiculously pompous' rendering of 'incongruous platitudes'.[9] But he could relate a touching episode or sketch a war-picture with considerable vigour, and provides us with several insights into the rebellion which are not mentioned by other authorities. No English writer notices Sir Edward Woodville's advance on Doncaster and incongruous retreat through Sherwood Forest, for example, and only Molinet records how Lord Welles's panicky forces brought confusion to London. These were, probably, episodes which Tudor historians thought best forgotten, but the story would be poorer without them. Molinet did not question 'Edward VI's' identity and makes many errors of detail; but it is likely that some of his information came from one or more of Schwartz's soldiers who had escaped back to the Continent, or from inquiries made by Duchess Margaret. We will probably never know if 'Scanfort' is Carnforth, Castleford or Stainforth (or any of them), but some aspects of his testimony cannot be ignored.

These are our principal sources for the rebellion and battle, but there are others, briefer or more derivative, which still offer particular insights. The earliest is the 'life' of Henry VII written by his blind poet laureate, Bernard André, probably *c.*1500–1502. André was a well-educated Augustinian friar, a native of Toulouse, who probably met Henry on the Continent and came with him to England in 1485. He was appointed tutor to Prince Arthur, Henry's eldest son, and also taught at Oxford, but in 1500 retired from court to study with the intention of presenting the King with a new literary composition every year. His *Vita Henrici VII* lacks much detail and extends only to the capture of Perkin Warbeck; but it includes a long speech which, he says, Henry made to his troops before the battle. This could be dismissed as merely a piece of poetic licence, but André also tells us that, when the Earl of Oxford made to reply, 'because time was pressing, the king proclaimed silence, and ordered attention to the exigencies of the time.'[10] A serious historian would not have invented a detail of this nature, and the same may be said of André's contemporary Robert Fabyan. Fabyan (d. 1513) was an alderman of London, a member of the Drapers' company, whose literary endeavours encompassed not only his *Concordance of Histories* (printed as *The New Chronicles of England and France*) but also the fuller and more informative *Great Chronicle of London*. It is, of course, highly improbable that a senior member of London society would have been privy to a terse conversation between Martin Schwartz and the Earl of Lincoln, but he could well have learned of it from someone who was captured after the battle and subsequently re-admitted to favour. Both men were writing *in* Henry VII's reign (as opposed to merely living in it and writing later) and their anecdotes have the ring of truth.

We might suppose that authors who wrote after, say, the first quarter of the sixteenth century would have nothing new to impart to us, but this is not necessarily the case. Edward Hall was a university-trained lawyer who held various appointments in London in the 1530s and 1540s. His *Union of the two noble and illustre families of Lancaster and York* (printed posthumously in 1548), is primarily a panegyric describing how the Tudors had rescued England from a century of strife and turmoil, and large portions of his account of Henry VII's reign are copied (i.e. translated) from Polydore Vergil. But he also had access to sources now lost to us, and it is from him that we learn that the King 'was in hys (Lincoln's) bosome and knewe every houre what the Erle did.'[11] Still further removed in time is Francis Bacon's *History of the Reign of King Henry VII* which the author dedicated and presented to Prince Charles (who, as King, was destined to die on the scaffold) in March 1622. Bacon derived much of his information from Hall and did not always adhere to his own high precepts of scholarship; but his book was, in the words of a recent editor, 'the first classic of English historical writing'[12] and the first in-depth discussion of Henry's reign composed after the death of the last ruler of the dynasty. Bacon could state what Vergil could only imply – that Elizabeth Woodville had been punished for her involvement in the Simnel conspiracy – and is the first writer to suggest that Lovel escaped from the battlefield and 'lived long after in a cave or vault'.[13] The sixteenth-century *Book of Howth* tells a similar story to Polydore Vergil, but from it we learn that Nicholas, afterwards Lord Howth, kept Henry informed of events in Ireland after Simnel arrived there, and how the King poked fun at the Irish nobles who had recognised the pretender when he summoned them to England in 1489. The list is by no means exhaustive – there are sources ranging from bishops' registers to private letters which furnish perhaps a single detail or insight – but collectively (and within their limitations) they allow at least some pieces of the jig-saw to be put in place.

We are almost entirely dependent on the literary sources for our knowledge of events leading up to 16 June 1487, but can look to archaeology for help in reconstructing the battle and its aftermath. Weapons and armour were prized and scavengers would have carried away everything of value, but the remaining debris, including the near-naked bodies of most of those who had fallen, would have been disposed of on site. Grave pits are likely to have been dug close to the areas of the greatest carnage, in this case, where the two vanguards fought much of the battle, in various places to the rear and north where fugitives were caught and cut down as they tried to escape their pursuers, and near the rebel baggage-train, which would have been thoroughly looted. We would also expect to find arrow-heads and gun-shot in the first of these locations (if the acidity of the soil has allowed the iron to survive the intervening five centuries) with perhaps more general rubbish in the third. The older discoveries are generally poorly documented and, to date, nothing had been found which would prove that the main battle occurred near Trent Lane or indicate the site of the baggage-train. But all the burial places of those who apparently fell in the rout that have been discovered are approximately where we would expect them to be.

When Richard Brooke visited Stoke in 1825 he was told that,

> 'human bones, coins and other relics indicative of a battle have been frequently dug up in the fields on the south side of the village, which are exactly where, from the accounts, it is to be presumed the Earl's (Lincoln's) centre was engaged, after descending from his strong post, which lie at the foot of the eminence (Burham Hill)'[14]

and that similar finds had been made when digging the foundations of some walls near the vicarage, just across the Fosse Way in Elston Fields. Sir Robert Bromley, the then-owner of Stoke Hall, showed him a place in his garden (near the western end of the medieval village)

> 'where the remains of many of the slain were found. They were interred in long trenches; but very few indications of armour or weapons were discovered; however the labourers found two spurs: one of which they purloined, the other Sir Robert Bromley obtained. He kindly allowed me to inspect it. It is of silver on the outside, and of steel within, and is of considerable beauty and elegance of work-manship. It is of very small size and remarkable for the appropriate nature of its ornaments – roses boldly embossed on its surface.'[15]

Brooke followed Vergil in believing that the rebels faced northwards while Oxford fought with his back to the village, and supposed that these were the burials of men killed in the actual conflict rather than in the rout which followed it. He was almost certainly wrong, of course, and perhaps did not realise that when his informants referred to discoveries in the 'fields on the south side of the village' they meant the area south of Burham Hill as well as in fields nearer to Stoke where a scatter-find was made at grid reference 475100/349500.[16]

Brooke also noted that bodies and artefacts had been unearthed in the 'Red Gutter', the gully in the steep scarp north-west of the rebel position, and another nineteenth-century historian, Cornelius Brown, mentions similar discoveries in what was then known as 'Dead Man's Field', to the north of the village where the Fosse Way joins the minor road leading to Thorpe.[17] It is likely that numbers of rebels were caught and slain as they scrambled down the 'Gutter' hoping to reach Fiskerton; but the story is traditional rather than specific, and may (as we have already noticed) owe something to the red Keuper Marl clay which has been extracted from it for brick-making at some time in the distant past. Similarly, we cannot say what, or precisely when, anything was found in 'Dead Man's Field'. It is possible that some fugitives were cut down here as they fled in the direction of Newark, but there has perhaps been a tendency to associate almost any ancient remains found in the area with the conflict. We do not learn if any of the skeletons had suffered battlefield injuries which would distinguish them from, say, plague victims, or whether the artefacts discovered with them were indisputably military or had everyday peaceful uses. Peter Foss has listed all the 'discoveries' made in the vicinity of Bosworth in his excellent *The Field of Redemore*; but few of them apparently relate to the late fifteenth century and the great majority are 'undated, unprovenanced and lost'.[18]

There is, however, one chance find which owes nothing to such speculation since it was uncovered only in 1982. Someone, possibly a metal-detector user, chanced upon an iron ring, or manacle, around arm bones in a ditch on the west side of the Fosse Way just south of Stoke village (National Grid Reference 475260/349460), and further investigation revealed the remains of at least eleven individuals in a cut 1.5 m long and 0.20 m wide. The skeletons were articulated, although the arms and legs were intermixed higgledy-piggledy, and there was a single skull which had apparently been damaged by a sharp-edged blade. A flattened area in the ridge and furrow of the adjacent field indicated that the burial pit was over 3 m wide, and many more bodies might be discovered were it to be fully excavated. The results would perhaps not match the recent discovery at Towton in Yorkshire (where the butchered remains of thirty-seven men were excavated in 1996, 535 years after they were slain in the battle), but they could hardly fail to add to our knowledge. It would be

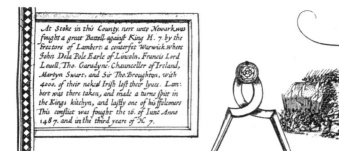

At Stoke in this County, nere unto Newark,was fought a great Battell against King H. 7. by the erectors of Lambert a conterfet Warwick.where John Dela Pole Earle of Lincoln, Francis Lord Louell, Tho. Garadyne. Chaunceller of Ireland, Martyn Swart. and Sir Tho.Broughton, with 4000. of their naked Irish loft their lyues. Lambert was there taken, and made a turne spitt in the Kings kitchyn, and lastly one of his falconers This conflict was fought the 16. of Iune Anno 1487. and in the third yeare of H 7.

Detail from John Speed's map of Nottinghamshire in his 1610 'Atlas'.

fascinating to know how many of them were veterans (i.e. how many had suffered skeletal injuries which had subsequently healed), and whether the lack of skulls was a feature of the whole grave. If so, it could indicate the mass execution of some of those captured in the rout.

There are techniques allied to archaeology which could – and possibly would – enhance our understanding of the battle and particularly the terrain over which it was fought, even if some of them are beyond the scope of the present inquiry. Analysis of soils and drainage could afford a better understanding of the distribution of areas of marsh, streams and of land usage in the medieval period, while more detail might be gleaned from historic maps and from aerial photographs of cropmarks and soilmarks, the former taken under dry conditions in high summer and the latter in the autumn. Existing aerial photographs, taken at various dates during the 1940s, do not, unfortunately, add much to our knowledge of the area, and the earliest maps held by Nottinghamshire Archives, made shortly before, and just after, 1800, are concerned with contemporary enclosures rather than with features in the landscape. They do, however, indicate some areas of older enclosure on either side of Church Lane and to the east of the Fosse Way which could have existed in 1487.[19]

This brings us to what must be described as 'informed guesswork' or what Colonel Alfred Burne famously called 'Inherent Military Probability'. His theory was that a medieval battle could be re-constructed by considering what an able and experienced commander would have done in such circumstances at any period of history, always assuming that nothing had changed in the interval. The problem, of course, is that things *do* change over five centuries, not only with regard to the landscape but also in terms of military theory. There is little point in discussing what a modern-day general would have done if he had been required to lead one of the armies at Stoke: we need, instead, to read the manuals from which men like Oxford and Lincoln learned to fight battles if we want to see the situation in their terms.

The most widely read military manual of the Middle Ages was Flavius Vegetius Renatus' *De Re Militari*, written towards the end of the fourth century AD. Vegetius was a financier rather than a professional soldier, but he recognised that it was necessary to deal with the barbarians who were threatening the Empire, and compiled a summary of 'best practice' which he culled from the military treatises of his own era. His book was amended and adapted by later copyists who sought to relate it more closely to their own situations, but it survived to become the standard work on the subject and was translated into at least six European languages between *c*.1250 and the end of the sixteenth century. Richard III possessed a copy – one of eleven of the first English translation made for Thomas, Lord Berkeley, in 1408 still in existence – and there can be little doubt that most, if not all, of the senior commanders at Stoke had studied it. Its great merit – and *ipso facto* the main reason for its success – was its straightforwardness and practical good sense. It dealt with recruitment, training and equipment, together with strategy and tactics, sieges and even naval warfare; but it never lost sight of more mundane matters such as keeping an army healthy, preventing mutiny, and handling troops who had little experience. Lincoln and Oxford would have been well aware of the need for subtlety ('There beth no counselles better then tho of which thyn ennemy hath no knowing till they ben doon in dede') and the desirability of keeping their armies moving ('Every hooste with travaill and labor profitteth and sutteleth, but with ydilness he dulleth'). They would also have known that 'Good Dukes ne fighteth never openly in felde, but they be dryven therto by sodeyn happe or grete nede', although in this case they were to have little alternative.[20] It is thanks to Vegetius that we can estimate the width and depth of the deployments of the two armies at Stoke (always assuming, of course, that our estimates of their numbers are reasonably accurate), and this gives us something on which to base our assessment of the extent of the ground they occupied and the particular problems this would have posed for them. It is not an exact science, but it is better than complete guesswork or no method at all.

There is, of course, always more that we would like to know, perhaps still more which may yet be discerned from the available sources, but the foregoing represents what, to the best of my belief, is the extent of our knowledge of the battle of Stoke at present. New documentary evidence may yet be found and the soil may continue to yield hidden artefacts, but until this happens – and until such discoveries can be fully evaluated – we must needs be content with what we have.

Appendix I

The Rebels of 1487

1. Rebels attainted in 1487. Source: Rolls of Parliament VI, pp. 397–400

John, Earl of Lincoln

Henry Bodrugan
Thomas Broughton, knights

John Beaumond
Thomas Haryngton
Robert Percy of Knaresborough (Yorks)
Richard Harleston
John a Broughton
Thomas Batell
James Haryngton
Edward Frank
Richard Middleton, squires

Robert Hilton
Clement Skelton
Alexander Apylby
Richard Banke
Edmund Juse
Thomas Blandrehasset
William Kay of Halifax, gentlemen

John Mallary of Litchborough (Northants)
Robert Mallary of Fawsley (Northants)
Gyles Mallary of Greens Norton (Northants)
William Mallary of Stowe (Northants)
Robert Mannyng, late of Dunstaple

Roger Hartlyngton
Richard Hoiggesson
Rowland Robynson
John Avyntry, yeomen

2. General pardons granted to Englishmen between 4 August 1487 and 11 August 1489. Pardons for specific offences unrelated to the Simnel rebellion have, of course, been omitted. Multiple domiciles and designations have been omitted in most cases. Source: *Calendar of the Patent Rolls: Henry VII, i, 1485–1494*, pp. 170–1, 175, 178, 191, 193, 196–7, 199, 202, 205, 209, 211, 222–3, 226–7, 236, 238, 250, 256, 258, 261, 264–5, 273.

George Ascu, alias Ascugh, of Nuthall
   (Notts), 'gentilman'
Thomas Ascu, alias Ascugh, of Nuthall
   (Notts), 'gentilman'
John Hibson of Stecnam (Yorks), 'yeoman'

Cuthbert Frere of Barton 'in le Willowes'
   (Yorks), 'yeoman'
Thomas Maners
John Barker 'gentilman'
John Hesple

Richard Rudforth
William Dobson
William Jakson
George Heryson
Nicholas Smyth
Roland Coke
William Gustarde
Alexander Lynsey
Christopher Lynsay
Andrew Car
William Coke
Thomas Clerke
John Brown
John Wilkynson
William Sandreson
George Porter, esquire
Thomas Mason, priest
John Maners
John Deplych
Edmund Coke
Arthur Borell
Robert Laveroke
Thomas Patansam
John Tempest of Gosburton (Lincs) &
  Brasewell (Yorks), esquire
John Aukeland, prior of Durham
James Hudelston of Estwite (Leics)
  'gentilman'
William Hamond of Kingston upon Hull
  (Yorks) 'marchaunt' etc. [with restitution]
George Carre of Alnwick (Northumb) &
  Horowdon (Northants), 'gentilman'
Robert Carre of Alnwick (Northumb) &
  Horowden (Northants), 'gentilman'
Nicholas Musgrave of Brakenthwaite
  (Cumb), esquire
Edward Musgrave
Ralph Bothe, archdeacon of York
William Claxton of Brancepeth (Durham),
  esquire
William Heslyngton, Abbot of Jervaulx (Yorks)
John Pullayn of Scotton (Yorks) 'gentilman'
Christopher Wellesbourne of Wycombe
  (Bucks) 'gentilman'
Leonard Redman of Burghwaleys (Yorks)
  'gentilman'
Robert Gower of Acclum (Yorks) esquire
Philip Constable of Flamborough (Yorks)
  'gentilman'

Peter Stanley the younger of Hoton
  (Cheshire)
Thomas Roos of Ingmanthorpe (Yorks) and
  John, his son, esquires
Richard Dukett of Grayrig in Kendale
  (Westmoreland), esquire
Alan Copeland of Santon (Cumb) 'gentilman'
John Hooper of Gatcombe (Glos) 'yoman'
John (Lord) Scrope of Bolton
William Preston of Gormanston, in Ireland,
  esquire
Dr Thomas Forester (or Forster) of London
Thomas Thorp of Wyvenoe (Essex),
  'gentilman'
John Menvile of Wicliff (Yorks) 'gentilman'
John Mallerey of Litchborough (Northants)
  'gentilman' (as 1 above)
Edmund Hastynges of Pykeryng Lyth
  (Yorks), knight
Thomas Metcalf of Nappa (Yorks), esquire
Thomas Hunt of Westminster, 'gentilman'
Thomas Goppe of Stirbrigge (Worcs) 'yoman'
Ralph Scrop, rector of Wensleye (Yorks)
John Rutter of Canterbury (Kent) 'yoman'
Robert Percy of Scotton (Yorks) [and
  restitution] (as 1 above)
James Harington of Thurland (Lancs),
  knight (as 1 above)
William Bothe of Elwik (Durham) 'gentilman'
Thomas Mauleverer of Allerton Mauleverer
  (Yorks), knight
John Buk of Plymouth (Devon), 'maryner'
William Wilcokes of London 'draper'
Roger Hastings of Pekeryng Lyth (Yorks)
Robert Tomson of London, 'taillour'
Robert Topping, alias Lyncoln, of Story
  (Kent), 'farmer'
Diggory Water, clerk
John Taillour of Exeter (Devon), merchant
  ('late a yeoman of the chamber to Edward
  IV and Richard III')
John Webbe of London, 'yoman'
Thomas (Lord) Scrope of Masham (Yorks)
Nicholas Palmer of Bristol, merchant
William Hogge of Gloucester 'tailler' [and
  restitution]
Anthony Thwaytes of London 'gentilman'
Roger Hartlyngton 'gentilman' (as 1 above)

3. Others

Queen Elizabeth Woodville
Robert Stillington, Bishop of Bath & Wells
Richard Redman, Bishop of St Asaph
John Sante, Abbot of Abingdon
Nicholas Boston, Prior of Tynemouth
Francis, Viscount Lovel

Sir Thomas Pilkington
Sir Robert Harrington
Sir James Harrington (?)
Oliver Frank (named, with Lovel and others, in the safe-conduct authorising them to enter Scotland in June 1488).

Henry VII's Supporters at
the Battle of Stoke

(Former retainers of William, Lord Hastings are marked with *)

Senior Commanders (J. Leland, *De Rebus Britannicis Collectanea*, ed. T. Hearne, 6 vols (1770), iv, p. 210)

Jasper Tudor, Duke of Bedford
John de Vere, Earl of Oxford
Edward Courtney, Earl of Devon
George Talbot, Earl of Shrewsbury
Edward Grey, Viscount Lisle
George Stanley, Lord Strange
Edward, Lord Hastings
John Devereux, Lord Ferrers of Chartley

Henry, Lord Grey of Codnor
John, Lord Grey of Powis
George, Lord Grey of Ruthin
Sir Edward Woodville
Sir Charles Somerset
Sir Richard Haute
Sir Richard Pole
Sir John Savage

Bannerets made at the *battle* (Leland, *Collectanea*, pp. 214–15 and *The Paston Letters*, ed. J. Gairdner (1904), vi, p. 187). Spelling modernised

Sir Gilbert Talbot
Sir John Cheney
Sir William Stonor
Sir John Arundell
Sir Thomas Cooksey
Sir John Fortesque
Sir Edmund Beningfield

Sir James Blount*
Sir Richard Croft
Sir Humphrey Stanley*
Sir Richard Delabar
Sir John Mortimer
Sir William Troutbeck

Knights made at the *battle* (Leland, *Collectanea*, pp. 214–15 and *The Paston Letters*, ed. J. Gairdner (1904), vi, p. 187). Spelling modernised

Sir James Audley
Sir William Tirwhit
Sir Edward Darell
Sir Amyas Paulet
Sir Edward Pickering
Sir Thomas Wolton
Sir Edward Norris
Sir Ralph Longford*

Sir William Sandys
Sir Robert Clifford
Sir James Harrington
Sir Robert Brandon
Sir George Hopton
Sir Harry Boulde
Sir Thomas Poole
Sir Robert Broughton

Sir John Devenish
Sir Maurice Berkeley*
Sir John Paston
Sir William Radmill
Sir Ralph Shirley*
Sir Thomas Lovell
Sir Gregory Lovell
Sir John Longville
Sir Humphrey Savage
Sir Thomas Blount
Sir William Littleton
Sir Henry Willoughby*
Sir Robert Cheney
Sir William Norris
Sir John Sapcote
Sir William Carew
Sir William Vampage
Sir John Wyndham

Sir John Digby
Sir Antony Browne
Sir Roger Bellingham
Sir Thomas Hansard
Sir Richard Poole (II)
Sir John Musgrave
Sir Christopher Wroughton
Sir Thomas Tyrell
Sir George Nevill
Sir Thomas Lyne
Sir Richard Fitzlewis
Sir Maurice Barrow
Sir Thomas Grey
Sir Nicholas Vaux
Sir Robert Ratcliffe
Sir Edward Burgh
Sir James Parker
Sir Thomas Manington

(Sir William Troutbeck has been omitted from the knights as he has already been named among the bannerets and Sir Thomas Manington has been added from the list printed in *The Paston Letters*.)

Others named by Polydore Vergil (*The Anglica Historia of Polydore Vergil*, ed. D. Hay (1950), pp. 22–3)

John Montgomery
Henry Vernon*
Godfrey Foljambe
Thomas Gresley*
Edward Sutton
Humphrey Stanley (II)
William Hugton
William Mering
Edward Stanhope
Gervase Clifton*
Brian Stapleton
William Pierpoint
John Babington*
William Bedyll,
Robert Brudenell
John Markham
William Merbury
John Hussey
Robert Sheffield
William Newport
Roger Ormston
Thomas Tempest

William Knyvet
Simon Digby
Richard Sacheverell
John Villiers
Edward Fielding
Thomas Pulteney
Thomas Green*
Nicholas Griffin
Edmund Lucy
Edward Belknap
Robert Throckmorton
Guy Wolston
Thomas Findern
David Philip
Thomas Cheney
Robert Cotton
John St John
John Mordaunt
John Rainsford
Robert Paynton
Robert Daniel
Henry Marney

Edmund Arundel
George Ogle
Ralph Neville
Richard Latimer

William Bulmer
John Langford
John Neville of Thornbridge
John William

(Rhys ap Thomas and Sir Henry Wyatt are also sometimes said to have been present, but are not named in any of the above sources.)

Appendix III

A Note about Lambert Simnel's
Irish Coinage

Lambert Simnel is almost unique among English pretenders in that, for a few weeks, he actually reigned over part of his dominions (Henry VII's writ only ran in Ireland when the Earl of Kildare chose to obey him), and because coins were issued in his name. Some groats were also struck for the next serious challenger, Perkin Warbeck, although these were produced in Flanders and have been dismissed by some writers as 'quasi medallic propagandist pieces'.[1] The probability is, however, that although never numerous, they were real coins struck in anticipation of the young man's invasion of England in 1495.

Simnel's Irish coinage consisted of groats and very rare pennies bearing a shield with the arms of England and France quartered by a long cross on the obverse and three crowns set vertically on a cross on the reverse. They are commonly known as 'three crown' groats for this reason. The obverse has the legend *Edwardus/Rex Anglie Francie* (Edward/King of England and France), and the reverse *Et Rex Hybernie* (King of Ireland). It is this last statement which has made it possible to associate the coins with Simnel since English monarchs always called themselves 'Lords' of Ireland until Henry VIII proclaimed himself King of Ireland in January 1542. There is no place for them in the Irish coinage of Henry's son, Edward VI, and so Simnel, who was crowned as 'Edward VI', is the only candidate.

The coins were issued in Dublin and, more surprisingly, in Tudor-leaning Waterford. It is unfortunate that they do not display a true-to-life profile portrait (a device which Henry VII may have adopted to distinguish his money from the issues of these pretenders), but they are a tangible reminder of the momentous events of 1487. It would not be surprising if Lambert always kept one in his pocket as a souvenir.

The Remains Discovered in 1982

The discovery of human remains in a grave pit on the west side of the Fosse Way (A46) just south the modern village of Stoke was mentioned in Chapter 10, and further particulars can be gleaned from reports prepared at the time of the partial excavation. The initial discovery was made at some time in the summer of 1982, but whether by a metal-detector user, or by County Council workmen employed to deepen the ditch, or by a metal-detector user *after* the Council workmen had deepened the ditch, is uncertain! Nothing was apparently done for several months (by which time it was difficult to re-locate the exact place where the remains were lying), but it was eventually decided to conduct a partial excavation in the hope of determining the age and nature of the grave and its occupants.

> 'It would not appear to be practicable to excavate the whole burial pit, but it would appear that it is possible to gather a good sample of the remains and [...] an indication of how they were buried by cutting back the slanting sides of the ditch – in this way 1–1.5 metres could be gained and examined with very little expenditure of time or effort.'[1]

The remains were deposited about 2 metres below present ground level, and the bones recovered and taken to Newark Museum consisted of 37 pieces of cranium; a piece of lower-right mandible with three molars and one premolar; an upper (?) mandible with three molars; 2 vertebrae; a proximal section of a humerus; a distal section of a humerus (right); 1 radius (left); 1 ulna; 2 pieces of radius and/or ulna (shaft only); 1 clavicle; 1 scapula piece; 5 metacarples; 2 pieces of rib; 3 pieces of pelvis; 2 left femur heads; 1 other femur head; 1 distal section of femur; 1 fibula head(?); 5 pieces of bone shaft; and 23 other pieces which could not be satisfactorily identified.

Several of the eleven partial skeletons recovered were examined in detail and the reports produced on them make interesting reading. Only the proximal half of the left femur of skeleton no. 1 was present, but the femoral head was clearly misplaced. It was high vertically, the head and neck were in line with the shaft, and there was an area of erosion and bony remodelling below the head on the anterior aspect. This could be taken as evidence of sacro–iliac osteophytosis; but none of the other remains showed signs of disease and the bony spur on the femur was almost certainly the result of stress caused by a congenital dislocation of the hip which had forced the victim to constantly limp. A possible explanation is that he had suffered from rickets, and that the resulting softening of the bones had led to hip displacement and shaft distortion. The same disability had caused slight bony growths and remodelling on two vertebrae (T12 & L1), but these were the only other features worthy of comment. Overall, the bones were apparently those of a youngish man who had suffered no obvious injuries when he died.

Not much of the individual who forms the subject of report no. 3 was present, but his was the only skull found in the pit. He had well–defined brows and a square chin, but although aged only 'about 20' his upper first incisor teeth were badly chipped and worn. The same wear and tear had made his upper second incisors 'shovel shaped', and his problems were compounded by a malformation affecting the lingual side of the right tooth which caused an overbite evidenced by the polish on the back. Hairline fractures radiating from the front of the frontal bone of the skull could have been caused by a blow to the forehead or by post–mortem pressure, but there can be no doubt that two wounds on the right side of the head were the result of blows struck with a heavy, sharp–edged weapon, one of which, above the ear, could have been delivered from an angle as he was falling to the ground. Interestingly, one of these wounds ends in a circular lesion which may be an earlier healed trephination, and a small linear lesion on the back of his head had also partly healed. This was clearly not his first battle, but whether he had acquired his earlier injuries at Bosworth, in Schwartz's continental wars, or in a dispute in the mists of Ireland, will probably never be known.

The bones recovered were all 'clean' (i.e. there was no evidence of osteophytosis or arthritis), and had belonged to men who were generally healthy, well-fed, and of reasonable strength. There can be little doubt that they are the remains of some of those who perished in 1487, and it is something of a mystery why they have not been re-examined using up–to–date technology or why the authorities have not excavated the whole burial site.

Notes & References

References are given in full on the first occasion in which they appear in each chapter but in shortened form thereafter. The place of publication is London unless otherwise stated.

Introduction

1 R. Brooke, *Visits to Fields of Battle in England* (1857, reprinted Dursley, 1975). A.H. Burne, *More Battlefields of England* (1972).

2 Michael Bennett, *Lambert Simnel and the Battle of Stoke* (Gloucester, 1987). D.E. Roberts, *The Battle of Stoke Field 1487* (Newark & Sherwood District Council, 1987). M.W. Bishop, *The Battle of East Stoke 1487* (Nottinghamshire County Council, 1987). D. Beeston, *A Strange Accident of State: Henry VII and the Lambert Simnel Conspiracy* (Author, 1987).

3 See, particularly, A.W. Boardman, *The Medieval Soldier in the Wars of the Roses* (Stroud, 1998); M. Strickland & R. Hardy, *The Great Warbow* (Stroud, 2005). E. Cavell, 'Henry VII, the north of England and the first provincial progress of 1486', *Northern History*, 39 (Sept 2002); S. Cunningham, 'Henry VII and rebellion in north-eastern England, 1485–1492: bonds of allegiance and the establishment of Tudor authority', *Northern History*, 32 (1996); D.A. Luckett, 'The Thames valley conspiracies against Henry VII', *Historical Research* 68 (1995), and several important articles from *The Ricardian* listed in the bibliography.

4 B.W. Tuchman, *A Distant Mirror. The Calamitous 14th Century* (1978). Mrs Tuchman explains her choice as follows: 'The person (could not be) a king or queen, because everything about such persons is *ipso facto* exceptional, and besides, they are over-used; nor a commoner, because commoners' lives in most cases did not take in the wide range that I wanted; nor a cleric or saint, because they are outside the limits of my comprehension; nor a woman, because any medieval woman whose life was adequately documented would be atypical.' p. xiv.

5 Dr Bennett's *Lambert Simnel and the Battle of Stoke* is a comprehensive and spirited account of the rebellion, but sometimes makes assertions for which there is no evidence (e.g. that some of Lincoln's supporters joined him at particular places in northern England), and claims mistakenly that the Harringtons welcomed him to Hornby Castle, which they had been obliged

to cede to the Stanleys as long ago as 1475. These are, arguably minor matters, but they have been repeated by other writers since 1987 and are in danger of becoming 'facts'.

Chapter One

1 In *Anne of Geierstein*, chapter 7.
2 A. Goodman, *The Wars of the Roses* (1981), pp. 227–8.
3 H.E. Maurer, *Margaret of Anjou. Queenship and Power in Medieval England* (2003).
4 He was licensed to enter upon his inheritance on 6 November 1477, presumably his twenty-first birthday, (*Calendar of the Patent Rolls 1476–85* [1901], p. 62). He is elsewhere said to have been aged nine at his father's death in January 1465 (G.E. Cokayne, *The Complete Peerage* (1910–59), viii, p. 223).
5 Warwick had previously been granted £1,000 from the profits of Lovel's wardship and marriage to defray the expenses he had incurred in maintaining Richard of Gloucester at Middleham. See P.M. Kendall, *Richard III* (1973), p. 442, notes 1 & 5.
6 *Ingulph's Chronicle of the Abbey of Croyland*, trans. H.T. Riley (1854), p. 457.
7 W. Shaw, *Knights of England* (1906), ii, p. 19.
8 *The Great Chronicle of London*, ed. A.H. Thomas & I.D. Thornley (1983), p. 236. The full version is 'The Catt, the Ratt, and lovell owyr dogge Rulyn all Engeland undyr an hogge', the 'dogge' alluding, in all probability, to Lovel's crest.
9 *The Crowland Chronicle Continuations 1459–1486*, ed. N. Pronay & J. Cox (1986), p. 183.
10 *Ibid.*, The writer's comment that 'out of this warfare came peace for the whole kingdom' was somewhat premature!

Chapter Two

1 'And my lord lovell come to grace than that ye shew to hym that he pray for me', D. Williams, 'The hastily drawn up will of William Catesby Esquire, 25 August 1485', *Transactions of the Leicestershire Archaeological and Historical Society*, li (1975–6), p. 48.
2 *Letters and Papers Illustrative of the Reigns of Richard III and Henry VI*, ed. J. Gairdner, i (1861), p. 234.
3 *The Anglica Historia of Polydore Vergil A.D. 1485–1537*, ed. D. Hay (1950), p. 11.

4 *Ingulph's Chronicle of the Abbey of Croyland*, trans. H.T. Riley (1854), pp. 513–14. The herald who accompanied the court implies that Lovel and his men were dispersed before the King left Pontefract, and modern writers who follow him see the attempt to capture Henry in York as a later, last-ditch, gamble. But Vergil says that Henry only learned of the seriousness of the uprising on reaching York, and it seems more probable that Lovel tried to seize him while he still held the initiative.

5 Vergil, *Anglica Historia*, p. 11.

6 *Rotuli Parliamentorum*, ed. J. Strachey *et al.*, 6 vols (1767–77), vi., pp. 275–6.

7 *Calendar of the Patent Rolls: Henry VII, 1485–94* (1914), p. 94.

8 J. Leland, *De Rebus Britannicis Collectanea*, ed. T. Hearne, 6 vols (1770), iv, pp. 186–7.

9 The guarantees which these knights and others were obliged to find for the King are discussed fully in S. Cunningham, 'Henry VII and rebellion in north-eastern England, 1485–1492: bonds of allegiance and the establishment of Tudor authority', *Northern History*, xxxii (1996), pp. 42–74.

10 Although Mauleverer fell under suspicion the following year. See *passim*.

11 *CPR: Henry VII*, i, pp. 112, 119, 130, 133, 141.

12 Cunningham, 'Henry VII and rebellion', pp. 58–9.

13 *The Paston Letters A.D. 1422–1509*, ed. J. Gairdner (1904), vi, pp. 92–3.

14 *Ibid.*, p. 95. A correspondent told Paston in May that it was being rumoured he had met with Lady Anne Lovel, the implication being, perhaps, that the friendship between the Pastons and the Fitzhughs (Lady Anne's family), had interfered with his professional duty.

15 *Ibid.*, pp. 99–100.

16 *Rot. Parl.*, vi, p. 436. The allegation was not made until 1489, see D.A. Luckett, 'The Thames valley conspiracies against Henry VII', *Historical Research*, 68 (1995), pp. 164–72.

17 Vergil, *Anglica Historia*, pp. 13–15.

18 Michael Bennett, *Lambert Simnel and the Battle of Stoke* (Gloucester, 1987), pp. 43–7.

19 His father, Thomas Simnel, is described as a joiner, a baker, a cobbler, and an organ-maker in the various sources.

20 Vergil, *Anglica Historia*, pp. 17–19.

21 Francis Bacon, *The History of the Reign of King Henry VII*, ed. R. Lockyer (1971), p. 60.

22 Her will, drawn up shortly before her death, shows that she had nothing to leave to her surviving children or to pay for religious observances. Her quarterly allowance was probably taken by the abbot for her 'keep'.

23   Bacon, *Henry VII*, p. 55.
24   Some writers argue that Elizabeth was not involved in the Simnel conspiracy, that she retired to Bermondsey voluntarily and surrendered her lands to Henry as part of an amicable 'family settlement'. I deal with these points fully in my *Elizabeth Woodville: Mother of the Princes in the Tower* (Stroud, 2002), pp. 122–5.
25   For an excellent short biography of Stillington see *The Registers of Robert Stillington Bishop of Bath and Wells 1466–1491 and Richard Fox Bishop of Bath and Wells 1492–1494*, ed. Sir H.C. Maxwell-Lyte, Somerset Record Society lii (1937), pp. viii–xv. He was a typical absentee prelate. Professor Ross notes that he had only visited his diocese once in the twenty-six years he had been its bishop, but he exercised his rights of patronage even when under arrest. C. Ross, *Edward IV* (1974), p. 320
26   *The York House Books 1461–1490*, ed. L.C. Attreed (Stroud, 1991), ii, p. 737.
27   *Materials for a History of the Reign of Henry VII*, ed. W. Campbell, i (1873), pp. 172–3.
28   The correspondence between the King and the masters is printed in *Epistolae Academicae Oxon.*, ed. H. Anstey, 2 vols (Oxford, 1898), ii., pp. 513–23.
29   The phrase is Paul Murray Kendall's, *Richard III* (1973), p. 475. It is sometimes stated that his imprisonment was permanent, but he was apparently at his episcopal manor of Dogmersfield in May 1489 and February 1491. *Registers*, p. xiii.
30   *York House Books*, ii, p. 542.
31   Dorset had shared Henry's exile for a time and Hall relates the allegations to this period, but it is more likely that he was suspected of involvement with his mother.
32   Bacon, *Henry VII*, p. 64.
33   Edward Halle, *The Union of the Two Noble Families of Lancaster and York*, 1550 (reprinted Menston, 1970), 'The politique governaunce of Kyng Henry VII', fol. ix.
34   Quoted by A.L. Rowse, 'The turbulent career of Sir Henry de Bodrugan', *History*, xxviii (1944), pp. 20–1.
35   *Ibid.*, pp. 25–6.
36   For example, William Catesby's memorial at Ashby St Ledgers (Northants), installed *c.* 1506, states that he died on 20 August 1485 – two days before the battle of Bosworth and five before he was executed at Leicester on the 25th. This, in the view of Malcolm Norris, was 'a deliberate falsehood to obscure the circumstances of (his) death'. M. Norris,

'Catesby brasses at Ashby St Legers' (sic), *The Ricardian*, ii (1972), pp. 28–32.

Chapter Three

1 These were Thomas Batell, Edmund Juse, and Thomas Blandrehasset of Greenwich, Kent.

2 *Calendar of the Patent Rolls: Henry VII, 1485–1494* (1914), pp. 119, 130.

3 F.P. Barnard, *Edward IV's French Expedition of 1475* (Gloucester, 1975). p. 98. His kinswoman, Jane, Lady Pilkington, bequeathed him her moiety of Balderton since he had 'no livelod'. Dr Horrox mentions a 'family tradition' that he was killed at Bosworth (*Oxford Dictionary of National Biography*, ed. H.C.G. Matthew & B. Harrison, 60 vols [Oxford, 2004], xxv, p. 385) – perhaps later generations thought this more honourable than falling on hard times?

4 *The Plumpton Letters and Papers*, ed. J. Kirby (Cambridge, 1996), p. 71. See also *British Library Harleian Manuscript*, ed. R. Horrox & P.W. Hammond, 4 vols (1979–83), i., p. 287.

5 *CPR: Henry VII*, i, p. 60. S. Cunningham, 'Henry VII and rebellion in north-eastern England 1485–1492: bonds of allegiance and the establishment of Tudor authority'. *Northern History*, 32 (1996), p. 65. He had, in the meantime, been appointed surveyor of Middleham in August 1486, *CPR: Henry VII*, i, p. 130.

6 He had received grants from Richard III and had been confirmed in his office of master forester of Pickering by Henry VII. Cunningham, 'Henry VII and rebellion' p. 63.

7 See Appendix 1. The list contains 81 names, but ten of these, Pullen, the two Lords Scrope, J. Mallary, E. Hastings, T. Metcalf, Percy, J. Harrington the younger, Mauleverer, & Hartlington, are noticed separately. It can only be approximate – some will have been pardoned for offences unrelated to the Simnel rebellion while others who were involved may not have been forgiven until later – but it is probably no less accurate than many figures culled from the medieval age.

8 See Appendix 2.

9 Cunningham, 'Henry VII and rebellion', p. 61. He was pardoned in June 1488 (*CPR: Henry VII*, i, p. 225) and his bond cancelled for his 'true service doon unto us' in November 1492.

10 W.E. Hampton writes that 'the custom (now rarely performed) is known as "riding the Black Lad"' and concludes with the destruction of the effigy. Sir Ralph must have made a profound impression on his contemporaries – a

northern Bodrugan, perhaps? W.E. Hampton, *Memorials of the Wars of the Roses* (Upminster, 1979), pp. 101–2.

11 Historical Manuscripts Commission, *Report on the Manuscripts of the late Reginald Rawdon Hastings of The Manor House, Ashby de la Zouch*, 78, i (1928), pp. 3 & 296.

12 K.B. McFarlane, *England in the Fifteenth Century* (1981), p. 250 and notes 50 & 51. *British Library Harleian Manuscript 433*, ii, p. 53.

13 The agreement is preserved in *British Library Harleian Manuscript 3881*, fos. 24 & 24d.

14 The Lovel family's links with Titchmarsh in Northamptonshire would have helped to make Francis acceptable to the county communities in the area – a major consideration.

15 This section is based upon I. Grimble, *The Harrington Family* (1957), pp. 51–61.

16 C.S.L. Davies, 'Richard III, Henry VII & the Island of Jersey', *The Ricardian*, ix (1992), p. 339.

17 *Materials for a History of the Reign of Henry VII*, ed. W. Campbell, i (1873), pp. 186 & 372.

18 Quoted by A.L. Rowse, 'The turbulent career of Sir Henry de Bodrugan', *History*, xxix (1944), pp. 24–5.

19 *More's History of King Richard III*, ed. J. Rawson Lumby (Cambridge, 1883), p. 19.

20 *British Library Harleian Manuscript 433*, i., p. 149; ii., pp. 7 & 124.

Chapter Four

1 *York House Books*, ed. L.C. Attreed (Stroud, 1991), ii, p. 556.

2 *The Register of Thomas Rotherham, Archbishop of York 1480–1500*, ed. E.E. Barker (Canterbury & York Society, 1976), i., pp. 220–3. *Tudor Royal Proclamations*, ed. P.L. Hughes & J.F. Larkin (1964), i., pp. 12–13.

3 *Tudor Royal Proclamations*, pp. 13–15.

4 *York House Books*, p. 562.

5 *Rotuli Parliamentorum*, ed. J. Strachey *et al.*, 6 vols (1767–77), vi., p. 397.

6 An alternative suggestion is that the rebels chose an easier, but longer, route via Cartmel and Carnforth before turning northwards to Kendal or Sedbergh, but this is based on little more that the tentative identification of Carnforth with a place called 'Scanfort' by the Burgundian chronicler Molinet.

7 *A Shortened History of England* (Harmondsworth, 1959), p. 200.

8 *The Great Chronicle of London*, ed. A.H. Thomas & I.D. Thornley (reprinted Gloucester, 1983), p. 241.

9 *York House Books*, p. 570.

10 *Ibid.*, pp. 549–50, 555–6.

11 *Ibid.*, p. 571.

12 *Ibid.*

13 *The Anglica Historia of Polydore Vergil, 1485–1537*, ed. D. Hay (1950), p. 23.

14 J. Leland, *De Rebus Britannicis Collectanea*, ed. T. Hearne, 6 vols (1770), iv, p. 212.

15 *Ibid.*, pp. 210 & 214–15, and Vergil, *Anglica Historia*, pp. 22–3. The list of bannerets and knights given by the herald is replicated on two flyleaves of a copy of Caxton's *Game and Play of Chess* preserved in the British Library and has been printed by James Gairdner in the sixth volume of his 1904 edition of *The Paston Letters*, p. 187. The only variation is that there, Robert Ratcliff has been added to the list of knights while Thomas Manington has been omitted. Vergil gives the names of 66 individuals who joined Henry, but 11 of these are common both to his list and to the above, two are those of peers already noticed, and one, that of Henry Willoughby, appears to have been duplicated. The herald has similarly included Sir William Troutbeck among both the knights and the bannerets in his summary. A résumé of known royal supporters is given in Appendix 2.

16 See Appendix 2.

17 *York House Books*, p. 572.

18 *Ibid.*

19 The Croyland continuator notes, somewhat laconically, 'In the part (of the field) where the earl of Northumberland was posted, with a large and well-provided body of troops, there was no opposition made, as not a blow was given or received during the battle.' *Ingulph's Chronicle of the Abbey of Croyland*, trans. H.T. Riley (1854), p. 503.

20 *York House Books*, p. 572. Northumberland was at Richmond, in north Yorkshire, on 23 June. A.F. Pollard, *The Reign of Henry VII from Contemporary Sources*, 3 vols (1913–14), i., p. 54.

21 A. Goodman, *The Wars of the Roses* (1981), p. 104. Northumberland and Clifford remained in York only from Tuesday evening until about noon on Thursday, not 'over a week', as Dr Goodman implies.

22 This and the other quotations in this paragraph are taken from Leland, *Collectanea*, p. 212.

23 J.D. Mackie, *The Earlier Tudors* (Oxford, 1953), p. 73. The evidence of *The Paston Letters* may be found in volume 6 of Gairdner's 1904 edition, pp. 99–100.

24 Leland, *Collectanea*, iv, p. 212.

25 *The Great Chronicle of London*, p. 241. The writer tells how, 'by subtyll wayes men wer sett atwene the place of the ffeeld and many of the kyngys subgettys which were cummyng toward hys grace, shewyng unto theym that the kyng had lost the ffyeld & was ffled.'

26 Francis Bacon, *The History of the Reign of King Henry VII*, ed. R. Lockyer (1971), p. 68.

27 *Chroniques de Jean Molinet (1474–1506)*, ed. G. Doutrepont and O. Jodogne, 3 vols (Brussels, 1935–7), p. 564, translated by Michael Bennett, *Lambert Simnel and the Battle of Stoke* (1987), p. 131.

28 Leland, *Collectanea*, iv, p. 213.

29 *Ibid.*

30 *Ibid.*

31 David Roberts suggests that the rebels may have followed the Richmond–London road from Middleham travelling via Skipton, Keighley, Halifax and Rotherham to Mansfield; but they were too far east of Middleham by the time they reached the vicinity of Tadcaster for this to be a real possibility. D.E. Roberts, *The Battle of Stoke Field 1487* (Newark, 1987), p. 32.

32 Henry Tudor had maintained a similar speed before Bosworth, arriving at Dale on 7 August and approaching Shrewsbury, after a march of approximately 150 miles, on the 14th. He left Shrewsbury on the 16th and reached Atherstone, 55 miles away, on the 20th, an average of over 18 miles daily, notwithstanding that he may have deliberately eased his pace as he neared the King. See D. Rees, *The Son of Prophecy: Henry Tudor's Road to Bosworth* (1985), pp. 127–30, & M. Bennett, *The Battle of Bosworth* (Stroud, 1985), pp. 91–2.

33 Vergil, *Anglica Historia*, p. 23.

34 Edward Halle, *The Union of the Two Noble Families of Lancaster and York*, 1550 (reprinted Menston, 1970), 'The politique governaunce of Kyng Henry VII', fol. ix.

35 Leland, *Collectanea*, iv, p. 213.

36 M.W. Bishop, *The Battle of East Stoke 1487* (Nottinghamshire County Council, 1987), p. 8.

37 R.P. Shilton writes that 'at this season of the year the River is fordable by men, teams and cattle; and so very shallow was the water in the Summer of 1825, that on the first of August, boys not exceeding ten years of age passed and repassed in perfect safety. And on the 20th of June, 1826, the River at this place [Fiskerton] measured but 47½ yards in width and 21 inches in depth'. R.P. Shilton, *The Battle of Stoke Field, or Burham Fight* (Newark, 1828), p. 54. This matter is discussed more fully in Chapter 9.

Chapter Five

1 J. Gillingham, *The Wars of the Roses* (1981), p. 242.

2 M.K. Jones, *Bosworth 1485: Psychology of a Battle* (Stroud, 2002), pp. 14, 107–8, 164.

3 Glenn Foard, writing on the Battlefields Trust UK Battlefields Resource Centre website (www.battlefieldstrust.com/resource-centre) notes that 'though the ridge and furrow of the medieval field system has long since gone, there is still good archaeological evidence which should allow the reconstruction of the medieval landscape of the battlefield.'

4 J. Leland, *De Rebus Britannicis Collectanea*, ed. T. Hearne, 6 vols (1770), iv, p. 214.

5 Michael K. Jones has recently tried to re-locate the action to a site near Atherstone, 8 miles from the traditional battlefield. Jones, *Bosworth 1485*, pp. 149–157.

6 *Rotuli Parliamentorum*, ed. J. Strachey *et al.*, 6 vols (1767–77), vi., p. 397. *The Great Chronicle of London*, ed. A.H. Thomas & I.D. Thornley (1983), p. 241. *The Book of Howth* in *Calendar of the Carew Manuscripts*, ed. J.S. Brewer & W. Bullen, v (1871), p. 189. *York House Books*, ed. L.C. Attreed (Stroud, 1991), ii, p. 573.

7 *Chroniques de Jean Molinet (1474–1506)*, ed. G. Doutrepont and O. Jodogne, 3 vols (Brussels, 1935–7), i, p. 565, translated by Michael Bennett, *Lambert Simnel and the Battle of Stoke* (Gloucester, 1987), p. 131. Leland, *Collectanea*, iv, p. 214.

8 R.P. Shilton, *The Battle of Stoke Field, or Burham Fight* (Newark, 1828), p. 64.

9 However, Glenn Foard, writing on the UK Battlefields Resource Centre website (see note 3), suggests that the rebels may have been drawn up on an area of heath or moor known as Flintham Lings, just over two miles south-west of Stoke village. The association with Stoke derives, he suggests, from their retreat and the slaughter which ensued when they found their way restricted by the enclosure around the village. This deserves fuller investigation, but it is surprising that no contemporary or near-contemporary writer mentions Flintham if the main fighting occurred there.

10 Ariel photographs taken in the 1940s reveal no trace of the Upper Fosse or the ridge and furrow of the medieval open field furlongs; but some remains of the house platforms and boundaries of the former village (partially de-populated by plague in the seventeenth century) may still be seen on either side of Church Lane.

11 Francis Bacon, *The History of the Reign of King Henry VII*, ed. R. Lockyer (1971), p. 66.

12 See, for example, M. Bennett, *Lambert Simnel and the Battle of Stoke* (Gloucester, 1987), p. 95. D.E. Roberts, *The Battle of Stoke Field 1487* (Newark, 1987), Appendix 1, pp. 65–6. G. Foard, *UK Battlefields Resource Centre Website* (www.battlefieldstrust.com/resource-centre), 'The Armies & the Losses'.

13 Even knightly contingents could be substantial in the right circumstances. Sir Walter Strickland of Sizergh (Cumb.) promised to serve the Earl of Salisbury with 69 archers and 74 billmen horsed and harnessed and 71 archers and 76 billmen not so equipped, in 1448, while Sir Gilbert Talbot raised 500 men from his own lands and from the estates of his nephew, the Earl of Shrewsbury, before Bosworth in 1485.

14 *Memorials of King Henry VIII*, ed. J. Gairdner (1858), p. 51, translated by M. Bennett, *Lambert Simnel*, p. 133. *The Anglica Historia of Polydore Vergil, 1485–1537*, ed. D. Hay (1950), p. 23.

15 i.e. 8,000 men divided by $6 \times 3\,\text{ft} = 4,000\,\text{ft}$. Vegetius estimated the *depth* required at 7 ft, so the line would have been 35 ft deep.

16 Molinet in Bennett, *Lambert Simnel* , p. 131. I have assumed an *average* depth of six ranks when calculating the length of Oxford's line since more troops were clearly allocated to Sir Edward Woodville on the vulnerable right wing than to Sir John Savage on the left. Cavalry units were used in some Wars of the Roses battles, but for lack of evidence to the contrary I have assumed that, until some mounted reinforcements arrived or until hot pursuit became necessary, both armies at Stoke fought on foot.

17 G. Foard, *Bosworth Battlefield: A Reassessment*, unpublished report prepared for Leicestershire County Council, 2004. I am grateful for permission to use this.

18 Bacon, *Henry VII*, p. 67.

19 Vergil, *Anglica Historia*, p. 23. Charles the Bold, the last Valois duke of Burgundy, was a great general on paper, but his mongrel armies, which included troops drawn from Flanders, Holland, Picardy and Italy as well as Burgundy, always lacked cohesion and disintegrated in the face of determined assaults.

20 Jean de Bueil, *Le Jouvencel*, ed. L. Lecestre, 2 vols (Paris, 1887–9), i., p. 153, quoted in P. Contamine, *War in the Middle Ages* (Oxford, 1984), p. 231.

21 *Ibid.*, Leland, *Collectanea*, iv, p. 214. The herald is here referring to Oxford's deployments but it would have been no less true of the rebels.

22 This reconstruction is based upon figures given in A.W. Boardman's *The Medieval Soldier in The Wars of the Roses* (Stroud, 1998), especially pp. 120, 142, 145, 147, & 152–3. There is also much useful information in

M. Strickland and R. Hardy, *The Great Warbow* (Stroud, 2005), especially chapters 16 & 19.

23 Molinet in Bennett, *Lambert Simnel*, p. 131; Edward Halle, *The Union of the Two Noble Families of Lancaster and York*, 1550 (reprinted Menston, 1970), 'The politique governaunce of Kyng Henry VII', fol. x.

24 Vergil, *Anglica Historia*, p. 23.

25 It is also probable that, unless the battle line moved significantly, the numbers of those killed or severely wounded would have begun to hamper the movements of their colleagues who were still fighting unless there was an opportunity to move some of them to the rear.

26 *Three Books of Polydore Vergil's English History*, ed. H. Ellis (1844), p. 224.

27 Vergil, *Anglica Historia*, p. 23

28 It is sometimes argued that archers operated only from the wings in medieval battles, but the broad fronts employed would have made it impossible for them to hit combatants at the centre of the line with their arrows if this had been the case at Stoke.

29. Sir Walter Strickland had supplied the Earl of Salisbury with nearly as many bowmen as billmen (see note 13), and the overall ratio in the forces which Edward IV took to France in 1475 was seven archers to one man-at-arms. Strickland & Hardy, *The Great Warbow*, p. 380.

30 This estimate is based on an assumed marching speed of 3 miles per hour. It would have taken the rebels approximately five minutes to cover the full quarter-mile between the ridge and Trent Lane.

31 *York House Books*, ii, p. 573.

32 Hall's *Chronicle*, fol. x.

33 Leland, *Collectanea*, iv, p. 214.

34 Molinet in Bennett, *Lambert Simnel*, p. 131.

Chapter Six

1 *Chroniques de Jean Molinet (1474–1506)*, ed. G. Doutrepont and O. Jodogne, 3 vols (Brussels, 1935–7), i, p. 565, translated by Michael Bennett, *Lambert Simnel and the Battle of Stoke* (Gloucester, 1987), p. 131.

2 *The Anglica Historia of Polydore Vergil, 1485–1537*, ed. D. Hay (1950), p. 27.

3 *Letters and Papers Illustrative of the Reigns of Richard III and Henry VII*, ed. J. Gairdner, i (1861), pp. 94–6. Translated in A.F. Pollard, *The Reign of Henry VII from Contemporary Sources*, iii (1914), pp. 156–7.

4 This is fully discussed in D. Baldwin, *Elizabeth Woodville: Mother of the Princes in the Tower* (Stroud, 2002), pp. 122–5 & 132–7.

5 See S. Cunningham, 'Henry VII and rebellion in north-eastern England 1485–1492: bonds of allegiance and the establishment of Tudor authority'.

Northern History, 32 (1996), p. 65. The Prior of Durham was pardoned on 20 August 1487, and the Archdeacon of York and the Abbot of Jervaulx on 24 August.

6 Cunningham, 'Henry VII and rebellion', pp. 64 & 73. *Calendar of the Patent Rolls: Henry VII 1485–1494* (1914), pp. 190, 199, 273. G.E. Cokayne & others. *The Complete Peerage*, xi (1949), pp. 544–6. His sureties were Sir Robert Clifford of Aspenden (Herts), Sir John Everingham of Birkin (Yorks), Sir Robert Ryther of Ryther (Yorks), and Sir William Mallory of Studley Royal (Yorks).

7 Cunningham, 'Henry VII and rebellion', pp. 64 & 73. *CPR: Henry VII*, i., p. 238 & 264. *Complete Peerage*, xi, pp. 569–70. His sureties, who also agreed to be bound in the sum of £2,000 each, were Sir James Strangeways of Whorlton (Yorks), Sir Thomas Fitzwilliam of Aldwark (Yorks), and John Huddleston of Sudeley (Glos.), esquire. He was formally pardoned on 18 February 1489.

8 Cunningham, 'Henry VII and rebellion', p. 64. *CPR: Henry VII*, i., pp. 209 & 242. *Materials for a History of the Reign of Henry VII*, ed. W. Campbell, ii., (1877) p. 442. His sureties included his brother Sir Hugh Hastings of Fenwick (Yorks) together with John Everingham and Robert Ryther, who also acted as mainpernors for John Scrope.

9 Bennett, *Lambert Simnel*, p. 150, note 27. Frank was clearly free when he was asked to look for Lord Lovel before February 1488.

10 Campbell, *Materials*, ii., p. 330.

11 *CPR: Henry VII*, i., pp. 208, 222, 271, 273. Campbell, *Materials*, ii., pp. 187, 401, 521. PRO, *36th Report of the Deputy Keeper* (1875), Appendix 1, p. 20. My thanks to Ann Wroe for this reference.

12 *CPR: Henry VII*, i., pp. 316 & 466. The identification of these men must necessarily be tentative, but they bear the same names as two of the rebels and satisfy the requirements of time and place.

13 These particulars are taken from W.E. Hampton, *Memorials of the Wars of the Roses* (Upminster, 1979), p. 242.

14 Campbell, *Materials*, ii., pp. 256–7.

15 See A. Wroe, *Perkin* (2004), pp. 91, 137, 234, 253, 239, 292, 298, 332.

16 E.L. O'Brien in the *Oxford Dictionary of National Biography*, ed. H.C.G. Matthew & B. Harrison, xxv (Oxford, 2004), p. 328.

17 E.W. Ives, '"Agaynst the taking awaye of women": the inception and operation of the abduction act of 1487', *Wealth and Power in Tudor England*, ed. Ives, R.J. Knecht and J.J. Scarisbrick (1978), pp. 26–30. The reconciliation was permanent. Bellingham married Margery, and his father-in-

law (who had been assaulted in the attack on Temple Balsall) bequeathed him his 'best silver cup' when he drew up his will in 1488.

18 PRO, *36th Report of the Deputy Keeper*, Appendix 1, p. 20.

19 The Pastons, with a father and two sons all called John, are perhaps the best documented example of such potential confusion – it is almost impossible to distinguish between namesakes about whom little is known.

20 Cunningham, 'Henry VII and rebellion', p. 68.

21 *CPR: Henry VII*, i., p. 227. This section is based on M.T. Hayden, 'Lambert Simnel in Ireland', *Studies: An Irish Quarterly Review*, iv (1915), pp. 632–7.

22 The clause in question has been lost from the document. One writer suggests that it bound them to forfeit their estates to the King if they rebelled again.

23 *The Book of Howth* in *Calendar of the Carew Manuscripts*, ed. J.S. Brewer & W. Bullen, v (1871), p. 190.

24 *Ibid.*, pp. 179–80.

25 *Letters and Papers, Foreign and Domestic, of the Reign of Henry VIII*, ed. J. Gairdner & R.H. Brodie, xv (1896), p. 542.

26 See. G. Smith, 'Lambert Simnel and the King from Dublin', *The Ricardian*, x (1996), pp. 498–536.

Chapter Seven

1 This chapter is an expanded and revised version of my article 'What Happened to Lord Lovel' published in *The Ricardian* in June 1985. I am grateful to the Richard III Society for permission to reproduce material used there.

2 Printed in J.O. Halliwell-Phillips, *Letters of the Kings of England*, i (1846), pp. 169–70.

3 Although Professor Chrimes sees no ulterior motive: 'The latter must have been sent very quickly, for the list of slain includes Thomas, Earl of Surrey, and the fact that he had not been killed must have been revealed very soon', *Henry VII* (1972), p. 51. P.M. Kendall, *Richard The Third* (1955), p. 467. Surrey was taken into custody almost immediately and his survival can never have been in doubt.

4 R. Arnold, *Customs of London* (ed. F. Douce, 1811), p. xxxviii. *The Anglica Historia of Polydore Vergil, A.D. 1485–1537*, ed. D. Hay (1950), p. 27.

5 I infer Morley's presence in the Tudor army since he was killed fighting for King Henry at Dixmude in 1489.

6 *Chronique de Mathieu d'Escouchy*, an extract translated by Gustave Masson, *Early Chroniclers of Europe: France* (undated), pp. 193–4.

7   Herald in J. Leland, *De Rebus Britannicis Collectanea*, ed. T. Hearne, 6 vols (1770), iv, p. 214. For the 'Historical notes of a London citizen' see the *English Historical Review*, vol. 96 (1981), p. 589. A similar notice in *The York House Books*, ed. L.C. Attreed (Stroud, 1991), ii, p. 573, indicates that the story was widely believed.

8   C.L. Kingsford. *Chronicles of London* (Oxford, 1905), pp. 276–9.

9   *Materials for a History of the Reign of Henry VII*, ed. W. Campbell, ii (1877), p. 556.

10 *Calendar of the Patent Rolls: Henry VII, 1485–1494* (1914), p. 134.

11 *Register of the Great Seal of Scotland*, ed. J.B. Paul (Edinburgh, 1882), p. 370. Sheilah O'Connor, 'Francis Lovel and the rebels of Furness Fells', *The Ricardian*, vii (1987), pp. 366–70. Two of the others were Thomas Broughton, who may also have been dead by this time, and Roger Hartlington who was pardoned a year later on 27 July 1489.

12 *York Civic Records*, ed. A. Raine, ii (Yorkshire Archaeological Society, 1941), p. 75.

13 *The Paston Letters A.D. 1422–1509*, ed. James Gairdner, (1904), vi, pp. 91–2.

14 *Ibid.*, p. 91.

15 N. Davis, *Paston Letters and Papers of the Fifteenth Century*, ii (Oxford, 1976), pp. 455–6.

16 Gairdner, *Paston Letters*, vi, p. 92. Edward Frank was indicted with Abbot Sante of Abingdon and others for his part in a conspiracy to free Edward, Earl of Warwick in 1489. *Rotuli Parliamentorum*, ed. J. Strachey *et al.*, 6 vols (1767–77), vi, p. 437.

17 A translation of the extract (in Latin) printed in *Notes and Queries*, 5th Series, x (1878), pp. 28–9. Curiously, there is no reference to this inquiry in the *Index of Inquisitions* published by the former Public Record Office (*Lists and Indexes No. XXIII*, reprinted New York, 1963), but Gairdner was surely too experienced a researcher to have been mistaken?

18 J.J. Bagley, *Historical Interpretation* (Harmondsworth, 1965), p. 268.

19 Professor Lander notes that 'Attainder was the most solemn penalty known to the common law. Attainder for treason was followed not only by the most savage and brutal corporal penalties and the forfeiture of all possessions, but in addition the corruption of blood passing to all direct descendants, in other words, by the legal death of the family.' J.R. Lander, 'Attainder and Forfeiture, 1453 to 1509', *Historical Journal*, iv (1961), p. 119.

20 *Rotuli Parliamentorum*, vi, p. 502.

21 Vergil, *Anglica Historia*, p. 27.

22 Campbell, *Materials*, ii, p. 550.
23 *Calendar of Inquisitions Post Mortem: Henry VII*, i (1898), p. 803.
24 *Rotuli Parliamentorum*, vi, p. 502.
25 G.E.C., *The Complete Peerage*, viii (1932), p. 225.
26 Both families traced their descent from William, Earl of Yvery, in Normandy, who died in 1155. See Burke's *Dormant and Extinct Peerages* (1883), pp. 331–2.
27 See *Notes & Queries*, 11th series, v (1912), p. 292. I am indebted to W.H. White and Geoffrey Wheeler for information concerning the likely deterioration of the remains.
28 Appended to his *Memoirs of Oliver Cromwell* (1740), p. 87.
29 *Notes & Queries*, 2nd series, xx (1856), p. 401.
30 *York House Books*, ii, p. 573.
31 J.R. Lander, *Crown and Nobility, 1450–1509* (1976), p. 140. G.E.C., *The Complete Peerage*, iii (1913), p. 294. The story of the 'shepherd lord' is first mentioned by Edward Hall, and, Henry Summerson, writing in the *Oxford Dictionary of National Biography*, comments that it 'hardly stands up to scrutiny'.
32 W.J. Monk, *Minster Lovell, Its Ruins and Its Church*, 2nd edition, with additions (no date), p. 15.
33 Bayly's poem may be found in W.J. Monk's booklet, pp. 13–15, and Roger's *Ginevra* in *Gems of National Poetry*, ed. Mrs Valentine (1895), pp. 29–30. It was too good a story to be confined to Minster Lovel alone!
34 W. MacArthur, *The River Windrush* (1946), pp. 151–3.
35 Historical Manuscripts Commission, *Rutland MSS.*, ii (1889), p. viii. I am indebted to Dr W.O. Hassall, sometime archivist at Holkham, for information pertaining to the records held there.
36 Francis Bacon. *The History of the Reign of Henry VII*, ed. R. Lockyer (1971), p. 67.
37 My italics. Cowper's remark indicated that the remains had collapsed as we expected.
38 *Rotuli Parliamentorum*, vi, p. 503.
39 *Ibid.*, p. 503.

Chapter Eight

1 *The Anglica Historia of Polydore Vergil A.D. 1485–1537*, ed. D. Hay (1950), p. 23.
2 The principle that a son or grandson should succeed his father or grandfather was well established by the late fifteenth century, but the situation was comparatively fluid if the king died childlesss. It is likely that

the mature and able Henry Bolingbroke would have been preferred to the youthful Edmund Mortimer (Richard II's closest male relative), even if the revolution of 1399 had not occurred.

3 A.R. Myers, *England in the Late Middle Ages* (Harmondsworth, 1952), p. 199.

4 *Ibid.*, p. 202.

5 *Ibid.*, pp. 209–10.

6 J. Harrington, 'Oceana', *Ideal Commonwealths*, ed. H. Morley (1901), pp. 203 & 223.

7 S.T. Bindoff, *Tudor England* (Harmondsworth, 1950), p. 53. I am indebted to Professor Lander for these quotations (J.R. Lander, *Crown and Nobility* [1976], pp. 296–7.)

8 Lander, *Crown and Nobility*, pp. 267–300 & 143. It is true that of nine peers attainted by Henry VII only one (John, son of Walter Devereux, Lord Ferrers of Chartley), secured *full* restitution of his properties: but Henry, overall, attainted 138 persons and pardoned 46, whereas Edward IV attainted 140 and pardoned 42.

9 The series of Acts passed against retaining in 1487, 1495 and 1497 typify Henry's resolution rather than (as J.R. Tanner has it) his ineffectiveness. (*English Constitutional Documents 1485–1603* [1922], pp. 8–9).

10 See D. Baldwin, *The Political Influence of the Hastings Family in the Midland Counties, 1461–1529* (University of Leicester M.Phil Thesis, 1990), pp. 165–72 & Appendix 10. Henry and his son also proved strikingly reluctant to restore noblemen who had supported the losing side at Bosworth however well they served them afterwards. Thomas Howard, for example, only recovered his father's dukedom of Norfolk after his victory at Flodden (1513) and never regained the estates which his family had been given by Richard III.

11 S. Cunningham, 'Henry VII and rebellion in north-eastern England, 1485–1492: bonds of allegiance and the establishment of Tudor authority', *Northern History*, xxxii (1996), p. 67. Northumberland was murdered near Thirsk while engaged in such a mission in April 1489.

12 Vergil, *Anglica Historia*, pp. 127–9.

13 J.J. Scarisbrick, *Henry VIII* (1968), p. 428.

14 This section is based on some notes made many years ago without indicating the sources. I apologise if anyone sees a resemblance between it and something he/she wrote themselves.

15 Creake Abbey, in Norfolk, a house of Austin canons, failed in 1506 when the last abbot (and resident) died and there was no one left to take

over. The Austin priory at Bicknacre in Essex ended similarly at about the same time.

Chapter Nine

1 R.P. Shilton, *The Battle of Stoke Field or Burham Fight* (Newark, 1828), p. 68n.
2 *Ibid.*
3 *Ibid.*, p. 54.
4 R. Brooke. *Visits to Fields of Battle in England* (1857, reprinted Dursley, 1975), p. 189.
5 F.A.A. Cotton, *A Pocket History of East Stoke* (Newark, 1987), p. 16.

Chapter Ten

1 *Tudor Royal Proclamations*, ed. P.L. Hughes & J.F. Larkin, i (1964), p. xxiii.
2 What Preston had called 'Liber 1' was no longer extant when Davies came to examine the records. His 'Liber 3' was subsequently retitled 'House Book 1'.
3 R. Davies, *Extracts from the Municipal Records of the City of York During the Reigns of Edward IV, Edward V and Richard III* (1843), p. vii.
4 *The York House Books 1461–1490*, ed. L.C. Attreed (Stroud, 1991), i, p. xvii.
5 *York Civic Records*, ed, A. Raine, ii (Yorkshire Archaeological Society, 1941), pp. 72 & 75.
6 *York House Books 1461–90*, ii, pp. 540–73 *passim*.
7 *The Anglica Historia of Polydore Vergil A.D. 1485–1537*, ed. D. Hay (1950), p. xxvii.
8 *Ibid.*, p. xxix.
9 G. Masson. *Early Chroniclers of Europe: France*, (no date), p. 270.
10 *Memorials of King Henry VIII*, ed. J. Gairdner (1858), p. 51, translated by M. Bennett, *Lambert Simnel and the Battle of Stoke* (Gloucester, 1987), p. 133.
11 Edward Halle, *The Union of the Two Noble Families of Lancaster and York*, 1550 (reprinted Menston, 1970), 'The politique governaunce of Kyng Henry VII', fol. ix.
12 Francis Bacon. *The History of the Reign of King Henry VII*, ed. R. Lockyer (1971), p. 20.
13 *Ibid.*, p. 67.
14 R. Brooke, *Visits to Fields of Battle in England* (1857, reprinted Dursley, 1975), p. 185.

15 *Ibid.*

16 M.R. L 1679. I am grateful to Virginia Baddeley, Sites and Monuments Record Officer at Nottinghamshire County Council, for supplying me with copies of these reports.

17 Brooke, *Visits to Fields of Battle*, pp. 188–9. C. Brown. *A History of Newark-on-Trent, being the Life Story of an Ancient Town*, 2 vols (Newark, 1904–7), i, p. 169.

18 See P. Foss, *The Field of Redemore*, 2nd edition (Newtown Linford, 1998), pp. 71–5.

19 The most interesting is a copy of an enclosure map of the lordships of East Stoke and Elston in 1795–6 (ref: DD1968/2) showing older enclosures belonging to Sir George Bromley.

20 A.F. Sutton & L. Visser-Fuchs, 'Richard III's Books: IV. Vegetius' *De Re Militari*', *The Ricardian*, vii (1987), p. 542.

Appendix III

1 See C.H.V. Sutherland, *English Coinage 600–1900* (1973), p. 121, n. 45. Warbeck's groats bore the legend *Domine Salvvm Fac Regem 1494* ('O Lord save the King') with the crowned arms of England on the obverse, and *Mani Teckel Phares 1494* (a version of the writing on the wall at Belshazzar's feast) with crown above lys and lion on the reverse.

Appendix IV

1 I am grateful to Virginia Baddeley for supplying me with these details.

Select Bibliography

The *Anglica Historia of Polydore Vergil A.D. 1485–1537*, ed. & trans. D. Hay (1950).

Arnold, R., *Customs of London*, ed. F. Douce (1811).

Arthurson, I., 'A Question of Loyalty', *The Ricardian*, vii (1987).

Francis Bacon, *The History of the Reign of King Henry VII*, ed. R. Lockyer (1971).

Baldwin, D., *Elizabeth Woodville: Mother of the Princes in the Tower* (Stroud, 2002).

Baldwin, D., *The Political Influence of the Hastings Family in the Midland Counties, 1461–1529* (University of Leicester, M.Phil Thesis, 1990).

Bagley, J.J., *Historical Interpretation*, i (Harmondsworth, 1965).

Barnard, F.P., *Edward IV's French Expedition of 1475* (Gloucester, 1975).

Beeston, D., *A Strange Accident of State: Henry VII and the Lambert Simnel Conspiracy* (Author, 1987).

Bennett, M., *Lambert Simnel and the Battle of Stoke* (Gloucester, 1987).

Bennett, M., *The Battle of Bosworth* (Stroud, 1985).

Bishop, M.W., *The Battle of East Stoke 1487* (Nottinghamshire County Council, 1987).

Boardman, A.W., *The Medieval Soldier in the Wars of the Roses* (Stroud, 1998).

The Book of Howth in *Calendar of the Carew Manuscripts*, ed. J.S. Brewer & W. Bullen, v (1871).

British Library Harleian Manuscript 3881.

British Library Harleian Manuscript 433, ed. R. Horrox & P.W. Hammond (4 vols, 1979–83).

Brooke, R., *Visits to Fields of Battle in England* (1857, reprinted Dursley 1975).

Brown, C., *A History of Newark-on-Trent, being the Life Story of an Ancient Town*, 2 vols (Newark, 1904–7).

Burke's *Dormant and Extinct Peerages* (1883).

Burne, A.H., *More Battlefields of England* (1952).

Calendar of Inquisitions Post Mortem: Henry VII, i (1898).

Calendar of the Patent Rolls, Edward IV, Edward V, Richard III, 1476–85 (1901); *Henry VII, 1485–94* (1914).

Cavell, E., 'Henry VII, the north of England and the first provincial progress of 1486', *Northern History*, 39 (Sept 2002).

Chrimes, S.B., *Henry VII* (1972).

Chroniques de Jean Molinet (1474–1506), ed. G. Doutrepont and O. Jodogne, 3 vols (Brussels, 1935–7).

Contamine, P., *War in the Middle Ages* (Oxford, 1984).

Cotton, F.A.A., *A Pocket History of East Stoke* (Newark, 1987).

The Crowland Chronicle Continuations 1459–1486, ed. N. Pronay & J. Cox (1986).

Cunningham, S., 'Henry VII and rebellion in north-eastern England, 1485–1492: bonds of allegiance and the establishment of Tudor authority', *Northern History*, 32 (1996).

Davies, C.S.L., 'Richard III, Henry VII & the Island of Jersey', *The Ricardian*, ix (1992).

Davies, R., *Extracts from the Municipal Records of the City of York During the Reigns of Edward IV, Edward V and Richard III* (1843).

Davis, N., *Paston Letters and Papers of the Fifteenth Century*, ii (Oxford, 1976).

Epistolae Academicae Oxon., ed. H. Anstey, 2 vols (Oxford, 1898).

Foard, G., *Bosworth Battlefield: A Reassessment*, unpublished report prepared for Leicestershire County Council, 2004.

Foss, P., *The Field of Redemore*, 2nd edition (Newtown Linford, 1998).

G.E. Cokayne, *The Complete Peerage* (1910–59).

Gillingham, J., *The Wars of the Roses* (1981).

Goodman, A., *The Wars of the Roses* (1981).

The Great Chronicle of London, ed. A.H. Thomas & I.D. Thornley (1983).

Green, R.F., 'Historical notes of a London citizen', *English Historical Review*, 96 (1981).

Grimble, I., *The Harrington Family* (1957).

Edward Hall(e), *The Union of the Two Noble Families of Lancaster and York*, 1550 (reprinted Menston, 1970).

Halliwell-Phillips, J.O., *Letters of the Kings of England*, i (1846).

Hampton, W.E., *Memorials of the Wars of the Roses* (Upminster, 1979).

Hayden, M.T., 'Lambert Simnel in Ireland', *Studies: An Irish Quarterly Review*, iv (1915).

Historical Manuscripts Commission, *Report on the Manuscripts of the late Reginald Rawdon Hastings of The Manor House, Ashby de la Zouch*, 78, i (1928).

Historical Manuscripts Commission, *12th Report, Rutland Manuscripts*, ii (1889).

Humphries, J., *Battlefield Hikes*, i (English Heritage, 2003).

Ingulph's Chronicle of the Abbey of Croyland, trans. H.T. Riley (1854).

Ives, E. W., '"Agaynst the taking awaye of women": the inception and operation of the abduction act of 1487', *Wealth and Power in Tudor England*, ed. Ives, R.J. Knecht and J.J. Scarisbrick (1978).

Jones, M.K., *Bosworth 1485: Psychology of a Battle* (Stroud, 2002).

Kendall, P. M., *Richard The Third* (1955).

Kingsford, C.L., *Chronicles of London* (Oxford, 1905).

Lander, J.R., 'Attainder and Forfeiture, 1453 to 1509', *Historical Journal*, iv (1961).

Lander, J.R., *Crown and Nobility, 1450–1509* (1976).

Leland, J., *De Rebus Britannicis Collectanea*, ed. T. Hearne, 6 vols (1770).

Letters and Papers, Foreign and Domestic, of the Reign of Henry VIII, ed. J. Gairdner & R.H. Brodie, xv (1896).

Letters and Papers Illustrative of the Reigns of Richard III and Henry VII, ed. J. Gairdner, 2 vols (1861–3).

Luckett, D.A., 'The Thames valley conspiracies against Henry VII', *Historical Research*, 68 (1995).

MacArthur, W., *The River Windrush* (1946).

Mackie, J.D., *The Earlier Tudors* (Oxford, 1953).

Martin, F.X., 'The crowning of a king at Dublin, 24 May 1487', *Hermathena*, 144 (1988).

Materials for a History of the Reign of Henry VII, ed. W. Campbell, 2 vols (1873–7).

Maurer, H.E., *Margaret of Anjou. Queenship and Power in Medieval England* (2003).

Masson, G., *Early Chroniclers of Europe: France* (no date).

McFarlane, K.B., *England in the Fifteenth Century* (1981).

Memorials of King Henry VIII, ed. J. Gairdner (1858).

Monk, W.J., *Minster Lovell, Its Ruins and Its Church*, 2nd edition, with additions (no date).

Moorhen, W., 'The Career of John de la Pole, Earl of Lincoln', *The Ricardian*, xiii (2003).

More's History of King Richard III, ed. J. Rawson Lumby (Cambridge, 1883).

Myers, A.R., *England in the Late Middle Ages* (Harmondsworth, 1952).

Notes & Queries, 2nd series, xx (1856), 5th series, x (1878), 11th series, v (1912).

O'Connor, S., 'Francis Lovel and the Rebels of Furness Fells', *The Ricardian*, vii (1987).

Oxford Dictionary of National Biography, ed. H.C.G. Matthew & B. Harrison, xxv (Oxford, 2004).

The Paston Letters A.D. 1422–1509, ed. J. Gairdner, 6 vols (1904).

The Plumpton Letters and Papers, ed. J. Kirby (Cambridge, 1996).

Pollard, A.F., *The Reign of Henry VII from Contemporary Sources*, 3 vols (1913–14).

Public Record Office, *36th Report of the Deputy Keeper* (1875), Appendix 1.

Rees, D., *The Son of Prophecy: Henry Tudor's Road to Bosworth* (1985).

Register of the Great Seal of Scotland, ed. J.B. Paul (Edinburgh, 1882).

The Registers of Robert Stillington Bishop of Bath and Wells 1466–1491 and Richard Fox Bishop of Bath and Wells 1492–1494, ed. Sir H.C. Maxwell-Lyte, Somerset Record Society, lii (1937)

The Register of Thomas Rotherham, Archbishop of York 1480–1500, ed. E.E. Barker (Canterbury & York Society, 1976).

Roberts, D.E., *The Battle of Stoke Field 1487* (Newark & Sherwood District Council, 1987).

Ross, C. *Edward IV* (1974).

Rotuli Parliamentorum, ed. J. Strachey *et al.*, 6 vols (1767–77).

Rowse, A.L., 'The turbulent career of Sir Henry de Bodrugan', *History*, xxix (1944).

Scarisbrick, J.J., *Henry VIII* (1968).

Shaw, W., *Knights of England*, ii (1906).

Shilton, R.P., *The Battle of Stoke Field, or Burham Fight* (Newark, 1828).

Smith, G., 'Lambert Simnel and the King from Dublin', *The Ricardian*, x (1996).

Strickland, M., & Hardy, R., *The Great Warbow* (Stroud, 2005).

Sutherland, C.H.V., *English Coinage 600–1900* (1973).

Sutton, A.F. & Visser-Fuchs, L., 'Richard III's Books: IV. Vegetius' *De Re Militari*', *The Ricardian*, vii (1987).

Tanner, J.R. (ed), *English Constitutional Documents 1485–1603* (1922).

Three Books of Polydore Vergil's English History, ed. H. Ellis (1844).

Tudor Royal Proclamations, ed. P.L. Hughes & J.F. Larkin, i. (1964).

Visser-Fuchs, L., 'English Events in Caspar Weinreich's Danzig Chronicle 1461–1495', *The Ricardian*, vii (1986).

Waters, G., 'Richard III and Ireland', *The Ricardian*, vi (1984).

Weightman, C., *Margaret of York, Duchess of Burgundy 1446–1503* (Gloucester, 1989).

Williams, B., 'Lambert Simnel's Rebellion: How Reliable is Polydore Vergil?' *The Ricardian*, vi (1982).

Williams, C.H., 'The Rebellion of Humphrey Stafford in 1486', *English Historical Review*, xxiviii (1928).

Williams, D., 'The hastily drawn up will of William Catesby Esquire, 25 August 1485', *Transactions of the Leicestershire Archaeological and Historical Society*, li (1975–6).

Williams, J.M., 'The Political Career of Francis Viscount Lovel', *The Ricardian*, viii (1990).

Wroe, A., *Perkin* (2004).

York Civic Records, ed. A. Raine, ii (Yorkshire Archaeological Society, 1941).

The York House Books 1461–1490, ed. L.C. Attreed, 2 vols (Stroud, 1991).

Index